D0516418

The Wisdom of Jesus

CONTRIBUTING WRITERS:
A. Boyd Luter, Ph.D., Anne Broyles,
Pamela T. Campbell, Theresa Cotter,
Larry James Peacock

CONSULTANT:
A. Boyd Luter, Ph.D.

Publications International, Ltd.

A. Boyd Luter, Ph.D., is associate professor of Bible at Cedarville College. He has authored or co-authored the books *Truthful Living*; *God Behind the Seen: Expositions of the Books of Ruth and Esther*; and *Women as Christ's Disciples*, among others. He holds a master's degree in theology and a Ph.D. from the Dallas Theological Seminary, and is listed in *Who's Who in Biblical Studies and Archaeology*, *Who's Who in Religion*, *Men of Distinction*, and *Dictionary of International Biography*.

Anne Broyles is co-pastor of Malibu United Methodist Church in Malibu, California, where her husband, Larry Peacock, serves as minister. She is an advisory board member of *Weavings: A Journal of the Christian Spiritual Life*, and she leads retreats throughout the country on a variety of family and women's spirituality topics. She is the author of many articles and books, including *Journaling: A Spirit Journey*, *Meeting God Through Worship*, and *Growing Together in Love: God Known Through Family Life*.

Pamela T. Campbell is director of publications for the American Association of Christian Counselors, where she manages *Christian Counseling Today* and *Marriage and Family: A Christian Journal*. She has authored numerous leader's guides, articles, curriculum guides, and books for Christian adults and youth.

Theresa Cotter writes for *Liguorian*, *St. Anthony Messenger*, and *Catholic Digest*, and has authored the books *Daily Meditations for Busy Grandmas* and *101 Table Graces*, among others. She holds an M.A. in teaching from the College of St. Thomas and an M.A. in religion and theology from the United Theological Seminary of the Twin Cities, Minnesota.

Larry James Peacock serves as minister of Malibu United Methodist Church in Malibu, California, where his wife, Anne Broyles, is co-pastor. His articles have appeared in such publications as *Alive Now*, *The Upper Room*, *Church Worship*, and *Weavings: A Journal of the Christian Spiritual Life*. He frequently leads retreats and spiritual workshops for the Academy for Spiritual Formation.

PICTURE CREDITS:
Front cover: **Archive Photos/Kean Archives.**

Back cover: **SuperStock:** "Three Angels" by Bartolommeo di Giovanni/Christie's Images (top); R. Dahlquist (bottom).

Archive Photos: Title page; **Art Resource:** Galleria d'Arte Moderna, Florence/Scala: 7; National Museum of Art, Bucarest/Cameraphoto, Venezia: 38; Uffizi, Florence/Scala: 14; **Corbis:** W. Wayne Lockwood, M.D.: 303; Charles Mauzy: 201; **The Crosiers:** Table of contents, 6, 47, 81, 91, 97, 106, 122, 128, 135, 165, 220, 245, 262, 281, 283; **FPG International:** Laurance B. Aiuppy: 224; Paul & Lindamarie Ambrose: 133; Charles Benes: 248; Color Box: 145, 147, 211; Gerald French: 172; Peter Gridley: 33, 287; H. Richard Johnston: 142, 153, 218; Richard Nowitz: 48; Alan Nyiri: 279; Richard Price: 55; Robert Reiff: 155; Ken Ross: 311; Frank Saragnese: Table of contents, 197; Robin Smith: 41; Telegraph Colour Library: 108, 242; Ron Thomas: 35, 127; **International Stock:** 174, 189, 209, 222, 225; Wayne Aldridge: 102, 239, 271; Kirk Anderson: 151; Scott Barrow: 111; Chad Ehlers: 69, 235, 300; Warren Faidley: 316; Bob Firth: 9, 30, 179; Ken Frick: 59; Andre Hote: 176; Kadir Kir: 23; Buddy Mays: Table of contents, 17; Johnny Stockshooter: 192; Tom Till: 19, 29, 93, 137, 167, 206; Hardie Truesdale: 78; **Richard T. Nowitz:** 194; **Zev Radovan:** 125, 214; **Rainbow:** Peggy Braun: 169; Dean Hulse: 159; Coco McCoy: 292; Dan McCoy: 208; Frank Siteman: 278; **Tom Stack & Associates:** E.P.I. Nancy Adams: 104; Scott Blackman: 87; Perry Conway: 65; Sharon Gerig: Table of contents, 57, 257; Thomas Kitchin: 228, 289; J. Lotter: 61; John Shaw: 290; Larry Tackett: 156; Greg Vaughn: Table of contents, 107, 251; **SuperStock:** 11, 21, 27, 66, 99, 101, 113, 116, 121, 139, 161, 188, 232, 246, 265, 295, 305; P. Amranand: Table of contents, 131; Arena Chapel, Cappella Degli Scrovegni, Padua: 284; Cappella Baglioni, Church of Saint Maria Maggiore, Spello: 241; Christie's Images: 182, 184; Civic Museum, Padua/Mauro Magliani: 199; R. Dahlquist: 76; Galleria Degli Uffizi, Florence: 89; H. Keller: 231; Maurltius: 71; Mia & Klaus: 25; Musee Ingres, Montauban/Lauros-Giraudon: Table of contents, 308; Museo del Prado, Madrid/Bridgeman Art Library, London: 44; Museo del Prado, Madrid/Giraudon: 260; National Gallery, London: 297; G. Outerbridge: 143; Rivera: 84; K. Scholz: 203; R. Uewellyn: 73; E. Van Hoorick: 50, 53, 269; P. Van Rhijn: 162; **Transparencies, Inc.:** Mike Booher: 254, 276; J.G. Faircloth: 62, 83, 95, 273, 315; Tom McCarthy: 237; Jon F. Silla: 118.

ACKNOWLEDGMENTS:
The publisher gratefully acknowledges the kind permission granted to reprint the following copyrighted material. Should any copyright holder have been inadvertently omitted, they should apply to the publisher who will be pleased to credit them in full in any subsequent editions.

The Return of the Prodigal Son: A Story of Homecoming, by Henri J.M. Nouwen, © 1992 by Henri J.M. Nouwen. Used with permission by Doubleday, a division of Bantam Doubleday Dell Publishing Group, Inc.

A Singing Faith, by Jane Parker Huber, © 1987 Jane Parker Huber. Used by permission of Westminster John Knox Press.

An Interrupted Life: The Diaries of Etty Hillesum, by Etty Hillesum, © 1984 Random House, Inc. Used by permission of Pantheon, a division of Random House, Inc., New York, NY.

God Holds the Future, by David Meece and Brown Bannister, © 1979 by Word Music (a division of WORD MUSIC). All rights reserved. Used by permission.

Copyright © 1998 Publications International, Ltd. All rights reserved. This book may not be reproduced or quoted in whole or in part by any means whatsoever without written permission from:

Louis Weber, C.E.O.
Publications International, Ltd.
7373 North Cicero Avenue
Lincolnwood, Illinois 60646

Permission is never granted for commercial purposes.

Manufactured in U.S.A.

8 7 6 5 4 3 2 1

ISBN: 0-7853-2555-7

Library of Congress Catalog Number: 97-75576

Contents

Introduction

Something greater than Solomon is here!
Matthew 12:42

Wisdom: The dictionary defines it as "knowledge of what is true or right coupled with good judgment." The historical figure that is most often associated with wisdom is Solomon. The Bible tells us that Solomon was unequaled in judging and mediating disputes.

Solomon is not the last word in wisdom, however. As brilliant and impressive as Solomon was, he and his wisdom will have to settle for playing a very beautiful second fiddle. For it is Jesus Christ who, after all is said and done, emerges unrivaled as the wisest person who ever walked the face of the earth. And walk he did—he faced many of the same trials and tribulations we face. He knew sorrow, and love, and grief, and happiness, and laughter.

The gospels of the New Testament, which tell of the life and ministry of Jesus, also record his incomparably wise words and actions. In the following pages, some of his words and some words said about him are interpreted by people from different walks of life. We have male and female pastors and lay people. We have writers of different denominations. The writers are at different stages in their lives. There are five writers in all, each with her or his own unique background.

Each writer offers a different perspective and a different voice—each gives us interesting and new views on well-known verses. But each has the same idea: They meditate on the words of Jesus and try to understand what he is saying

Let the Children Come to Me *by Carl Vogel von Vogelstein*

to us today—how he is giving us guidance and encouragement 2,000 years after his death. For the lessons in the New Testament are timeless—they speak to us today, just as they spoke to people hundreds of years ago.

The following pages provide insight into the wisdom of Jesus. They seek to inspire each reader when facing the nagging questions of everyday existence and the challenges of everyday life. Jesus offers his wisdom for everyone, both now and for the future.

When Jesus Asks You to Listen

Everyone then who hears these words
of mine and acts on them will be like a
wise man who built his house on rock.

Matthew 7:24

Action-Aimed Listening

In our society, breaking laws, such as the speed limit, is taken for granted, even considered cool. So how can a law-abiding person be considered great, especially in God's eyes?

Whoever breaks one of the least of these commandments, and teaches others to do the same, will be called least in the kingdom of heaven; but whoever does them and teaches them will be called great in the kingdom of heaven.

Matthew 5:19

To an increasing number of people, breaking certain "insignificant" laws doesn't matter. In fact, it may often look like the shrewd thing to do. After all, the police don't enforce the speed limit unless it's being exceeded by five or more miles per hour. Many schools don't dare enforce regulations on cheating unless it's an obvious major infraction, for fear of losing a costly lawsuit. Many businesses only pursue discrepancies so far because it is not worth it, from the bottom-line financial perspective, to spend any more for a relatively small return.

When you think about it, lawbreakers break down any society, little by little. Certainly that is obvious with those who have a total disregard for law and government. That kind of outlook is called anarchy and, whether intended or not, will produce utter chaos.

Sermon on the Mount *by Henrick Krock*

Lawbreakers are definitely a destructive force in a society. If arrested for their crime, they may have to serve time in jail. And, if the offense is serious enough, they may lose some of the privileges as a citizen of their country. In that sense, lawbreakers are definitely the "least" citizens of the society.

There is also the factor of example with which to contend. Onlookers, especially younger people, often model their behavior after those they consider exciting and successful. So, "teaching" is taking place by example, whether the lawbreaker realizes it or not.

Much the same is true in the spiritual realm. Those who break God's laws, even the seemingly "insignificant" ones, will be considered at the bottom of the ladder in God's kingdom. And the impact they are having on others' behavior will not be overlooked. The model of their behavior will be closely evaluated in the spiritual reckoning.

Sadly, law-abiding citizens in our country usually don't get the recognition they deserve. Because they do what they are supposed to do and quietly go about their business, they are generally overlooked.

Lord,
I have wanted to be great, but I didn't think I had what it takes. Forgive me for not realizing how you view greatness. Empower me to live out your gracious commands, and place before me the opportunities to tell others about true greatness in your eyes.
Amen

Happily, that is not the case in God's kingdom. In the Lord's evaluation of what really matters for time and eternity, obedience to his standards and passing on that reverence to others is considered true greatness.

Isn't that refreshing and freeing to know? You don't have to be the best to be great in God's eyes. All it takes is an attitude of obedience to him and a willingness to model this attitude to others. If you do these things, no matter your success in the eyes of the world, the Lord looks at you and says, "Great job!"

The Trusted Messenger

What does it mean to accept or to reject Jesus? How are we to respond to his message? Is God supposed to make a difference in our lives?

***

Whoever listens to you listens to me, and whoever rejects you rejects me, and whoever rejects me rejects the one who sent me.

Luke 10:16

***

No telephones. No fax machines speeding communication. No airmail service guaranteeing overnight delivery of correspondence. No e-mail or telegrams aiding negotiations or the rapid exchange of ideas. When the written word was used in times past, delivery of correspondence was often limited to the speed at which a person could walk.

Today, we respond with a shudder at such a glacial pace for dialogue and negotiation. Yet the people of long ago, despite their lack of technology, did develop a faster method. When someone wanted to communicate or negotiate with another, that person would chose a trusted messenger for the task. That messenger not only delivered the message but was actually empowered to speak for the sender. The words of the messenger were as the words of the sender; the exchanges between messenger and receiver were as the exchanges between sender and receiver. And the acceptance or rejection of the messenger was considered as being extended to the sender. Such was the custom of biblical times.

The Annunciation *by Melozzo da Forli*

In gracious harmony with such practice, the Creator-God sent the Incarnate-God as messenger. That Incarnate-God, Jesus the Christ, became one of us. Jesus walked this earth, spoke with us, ate and worked and laughed and cried with us while delivering the lasting message that had been entrusted to him. The rejection or acceptance of Jesus and his message were to be as the rejection or acceptance of God.

Today, however, our response to Jesus is more apt to be a tolerant acceptance rather than total rejection. With a lack of fervor, with a fear of risk, we often embody passive acceptance. We pose acceptance to Jesus with the indifference of a nod to a somewhat familiar face in the crowd; our reception of the gospel message may be indistinguishable from our response to a passed tray of appetizers.

But that is not how God desires us to receive Jesus Christ and his gospel.

You pursue me to the far reaches of my world;
You pursue me to the depths of my being.
And I, weary of the pursuit,
Slowed by my burdens,
Surrender in desolation,
Only to discover in you,
My God,
Freedom!

We are to receive the message with the enthusiasm of God's pronouncement concerning Creation: "It is good!" We are to receive Christ and the gospel with the faith-filled openness of Mary and her "Yes!" to the angel Gabriel. We are to receive the Spirit-inspired "Good News" with the fervor of those filled with the Living Flame at Pentecost.

We are to receive Christ with the loving joyfulness with which we welcome a family member who comes in peace. We are to receive Christ with the abandon of the saints and holy ones who risked all in the name of God.

The presence of Christ is to direct every thought, word, action of our lives. Such is the acceptance asked of us by our God.

Holy Ears, Holy Words

In the clamor and noise of daily life, Jesus blesses us for listening to him with our hearts as well as our ears. The key to life is found in hearing the word of Jesus in all the words and sounds around us.

Then turning to the disciples, Jesus said to them privately, "Blessed are the eyes that see what you see! For I tell you that many prophets and kings desired to see what you see, but did not see it, and to hear what you hear, but did not hear it."

Luke 10:23–24

I find it helpful to remember that hearing comes before speaking in a young child's development of language skills. In our noisy, talkative culture, we tend to overlook hearing as the foundation of communication. We focus on words and how to give them the proper spin, the right sound, the persuasive punch. Yet, in this passage, Jesus is commending the disciples and showering them with blessing because they hear what has been longed for throughout all of history. They hear the voice of love.

Hearing is a treasured gift from God. When we read the story of Helen Keller or see the movie *The Miracle Worker,* we are reminded that we should not take hearing for granted. Keller's deafness locked her out of the world of meaning and relationship. I am always deeply moved by the scene in the movie when Keller learns that the water pouring over her hand can be spelled in sign language. At age seven, she finally begins to hear (and see) with her hands—and the world opens up to her.

Our ears do open a world. They open the world of sound and communication. I remember a retreat leader urging us to put our hands on our ears and to offer a prayer of thanks for our ears. Our ears are always open. They bring the world to us. Physically, we cannot shut them to the world. We are forever in the posture of openness. They are one of the pathways that God uses to communicate with us.

There is a difference between hearing and listening, though. We may hear words or sounds, but not pay attention or seek to understand the

*Holy God,
Give me an inner stillness,
where the noise of the day
is smoothed by the tides of
your grace. Quiet my
anxiety, hush my chatter,
and give me enough silence
that I may dwell in your
healing presence. Give me a
heart at rest and open to
the sound of your voice.
Speak to me of comfort or
challenge, remembrance or
renewal, and let me forever
trust that you will lead me
on the paths of truth.
Amen*

message of the sound. Our ears may be open but our heart or mind may be closed to dealing with the information. My family has learned that when I am reading the newspaper, I am often absorbed in the story or events and probably will not hear what is said even if I nod my head or say, "Uh huh." I have to look up and face the one talking to me so that I can fully be present to listen. My ears as well as my eyes need to be focused on the one doing the talking. Listening is a skill to be developed; it doesn't usually come naturally to most of us.

Jesus addresses the disciples and blesses them for listening. The disciples are beginning to understand the content and message of Jesus—that he has come to reveal the love of God for each person. The disciples have just returned from a mission and have seen the power of God to heal and change peoples' lives. Their eyes and ears are beginning to grasp the incredible, forgiving, renewing love of God.

We are invited to listen to Jesus, to hear the Good News. We listen by reading Scripture, slowly and meditatively, as if hearing and reading a love letter. We listen to Jesus through participation in a church community, listening to the hymns, songs, and prayers; spoken words that hint at the very presence of God.

We listen to Jesus when we listen to a friend speak of their sorrow or pain and we don't interrupt with our own aches or simple advice. We listen to Jesus when we get down on a child's level to hear about their trip to the zoo.

Perhaps the clearest way we listen to Jesus is in prayer. We create the inner silence, the holy ground, where we can hear the still, small voice of God. Prayer is more than talking to God. It is also waiting for a word, a response, a nudge, a call.

As we develop the discipline of listening to Jesus, we will discover we are blessed. We will have our head cocked to the side and our ears tilted toward the sound of life. We will hear our own name called by God. We will begin to sense that we are God's beloved daughters and sons. We will know that we are forgiven and being made whole. We will touch our ears with gratitude and know deep in our hearts that we are truly blessed.

Hear and Now

If I took an auditory test every time my listening ability was challenged, most likely a hearing loss would not be the problem. I'm not hard of hearing, but sometimes I'm hard of listening.

He said to them, "If they do not listen to Moses and the prophets, neither will they be convinced even if someone rises from the dead."

Luke 16:31

"What will it take to get you to listen?!" Parents use this question to scold their children. Spouses use it to nag their mates. Bosses use it reprimand their employees. Teachers use it to discipline their students. Teenagers use it to irritate mom and dad.

What *will* it take to get us to listen? We all want to be heard or have a voice in matters that concern our well-being, but we live in a culture where good listeners are hard to come by.

So some people pay a mental health professional to listen for 50 minutes each week. Some hire lobbyists to make sure their concerns are heard. Still others freely share their stories on TV talk shows.

Our conversations often seem more like competitions. We don't have time to really listen to what the other person is saying, because we're too busy thinking about how we're going to respond.

In Luke 16:19–31, Jesus' story demonstrates what happens when people refuse to listen to him. When a rich man died and began to experience regret and the torment of hell, he begged Abraham to send someone to warn his family. But Abraham reminded the man that if a person's mind is closed, no evidence will change the person.

Listening is not an easy skill. But when we open our minds and hearts, we will be able to hear what Jesus has to say to us.

But the art of listening is something that all Christians need to nurture. God, in Christ, came among us as the humblest of human beings so that we would not be overawed and could freely speak of our brokenness and fears and be listened to.

Morton Kelsey,
Christianity as Psychology

God's Word Lasts Forever

In our easy-come-easy-go world, we long for something permanent to cling to. We know that all living things die, all situations change, and nothing remains the same forever… except God's Word.

✦✦✦

Heaven and earth will pass away, but my words
will not pass away.

Luke 21:33

✦✦✦

The world has changed drastically since the time Jesus walked upon the earth. It's hard to conceive of Galilee almost 2,000 years ago. Yet the humble man who spoke to shepherds, farmers, vineyard workers, and villagers continues to speak today to high-tech computer whizzes, CEOs of international corporations, politicians, and ordinary people like you and me.

How is it that words spoken to a particular people in a specific place long ago can still reach out to us? Why do the stories of Jesus transcend time and place, still finding a ready audience in our hearts? What makes it possible

*Whoever has God
Needs nothing else,
God alone suffices.*
Teresa of Avila

for us who live in the late twentieth century to understand the power of Jesus Christ?

Jesus was able to speak in images that his contemporaries easily understood: a shepherd looking for one lost sheep, a sower casting seed on the ground, a vineyard owner hiring day laborers, of lilies and sparrows. Yet those stories make sense to us today, as well.

The words of Jesus beckon to us across the centuries, reminding us that God's love has been with us always and will surround us even after we leave this life and enter eternity.

The words of Jesus call forth our best listening. Christ's stories mean nothing if we don't make the leap from "That sounds good" to "What does this mean for me?"

Jesus' timeless words make sense no matter who we are. As we grow and change, Jesus speaks anew. So we bring ourselves fresh to Jesus' word, knowing that its timelessness will always have a word of relevance for us if we but listen.

Degrees of Spiritual Fruitfulness

We all want to live fulfilling, fruitful lives. More than any other time in history, there are self-help materials that claim to say what that means. But what is spiritual fruitfulness and how do you achieve it?

But as for what was sown on good soil, this is the one who hears the word and understands it, who indeed bears fruit and yields, in one case a hundredfold, in another sixty, and in another thirty.

Matthew 13:23

Agriculture can be a highly frustrating occupation. If nothing else, there is the constant problem of weather. With crops or a garden, it is very common to have too much of a good thing, such as rain, sun, or heat.

Unfortunately, weather isn't the only variable that can make a huge difference in the success of a planting–harvest cycle. No matter how good the seed, it will not penetrate rocky soil and thus has no chance to take root and sprout. Also, hearty weeds can sprout alongside the newly planted seed and crowd it out. Nor is planting on good, fertile soil completely predictable. Sometimes the crop will come in moderately fruitful, though still successful. At other times, the product will be much more fruitful.

That is very much the way things are spiritually. If you are resistant to hearing and heeding the Scriptures, it is as if your life is rocky soil. There is no way the spiritual seed of God's Word can get a foothold.

If your heart is open to hear and apply biblical truth, your life is fertile soil. The question is no longer "Will I be fruitful?" Rather, it becomes, "Just how fruitful can I become by listening to and acting upon God's Word?"

Lord,
I truly desire my life to be
fruitful and productive,
especially in your eyes.
Please help me break up
any rocky, hard-hearted
resistance to you in my life.
Amen

Our Other Family

Family is of paramount importance in the Judeo-Christian tradition. However, as strong as those blood relationships are, there is an even more important bond. Faith can be more unifying than family.

And he was told, "Your mother and your brothers are standing outside, waiting to see you." But he said to them, "My mother and my brothers are those who hear the word of God and do it."

Luke 8:20–21

Many years ago when Vicky and David married, they made a commitment to live the gospel through dedicating themselves to the care of children. They raised 17 children, most of them adopted. All of those they welcomed into their home had known the rejection encountered by little ones born of mixed heritage or with handicaps. Eventually, their home became a microcosm of human diversity with its variety of races and colors and limitations.

When Vicky was interviewed about their lifestyle, she readily admitted that many people did not understand or approve of their commitment, including some of her relatives. Questioned how they were able to live in such a counterculture manner, Vicky answered, "This is our call and God has mercifully given us the grace to answer it as best we can. But, what is also important, we surround ourselves with people who support and affirm us."

Whenever any of us tries to live the gospel in all its radical, faith-demanding ways, we need the prayers and encouragement of

To belong to the family of faith is to inspire and to be inspired, to empower and to be empowered, to love and to be loved. We are to be as Christ for each other, both in our giving and in our receiving.

Christ and the apostles at the Last Supper.

others. However, family members can be among the last to recognize the Spirit calling us to a particular task or lifestyle. Thus we seek people who believe as we do, people who affirm us in our mission.

This is the example given us by Christ. When Jesus was fulfilling his ministry call, he too surrounded himself with those who affirmed him. And still today, Christ remains with all who respond to the gospel call.

I Hear and Obey!

Most of us like to make our own choices and act as we wish. The Word of God gives clear guidelines for how we are to live. How can we reconcile our desire for freedom and God's desire to guide our lives?

While he was saying this, a woman in the crowd raised her voice and said to him, "Blessed is the womb that bore you and the breasts that nursed you!" But he said, "Blessed rather are those who hear the word of God and obey it!"

Luke 11:27–28

When I worked with a group of Girl Scouts on their God and Family Award, we talked about how often they squabbled with friends and how hard it was to make up. I told them about the conversation between Jesus and Peter when Peter asked about the number of times we need to forgive.

*Trust and obey,
for there's no other way
to be happy in Jesus
than to trust and obey.*

John H. Sammis

The girls gazed at me as I asked them to multiply 70 times 7; "490!" one child replied. "So that's how often we are to forgive other people," I explained. Silence. The girls looked at each other, appalled. Then one girl spoke up, "That's too hard. I think I'll just ignore that rule."

Most of us have at least some rules we would rather ignore. Although Jesus gives us practical advice about living together, his words have little meaning until we put them into practice. Anyone can hear his words; it takes loving discipline to obey his commandments.

What are some of Jesus' words that are hard for you to hear? Look at these Scripture verses. Then ask yourself, "What point was Jesus trying to make? Why have these words been difficult for me to hear? Am I at a point where I can make a new effort to give Jesus my loving obedience?"

Spend time in prayer with these questions. Then choose one area you feel ready to work on so that you might be one of the "blessed . . . who hear the word of God and obey it."

When Jesus Asks You to Wait

Be patient, therefore, beloved, until the coming of the Lord. The farmer waits for the precious crop from the earth, being patient with it until it receives the early and the late rains.

James 5:7

Tested, but Not Testy!

It is often said, "When the going gets tough, the tough get going!" But there should be a caution light. It is easy to go off half-cocked and live to regret it later. How can you exercise patience in the midst of trial or temptation?

Jesus said to him, "Again it is written, 'Do not put the Lord your God to the test.'"

Matthew 4:7

When things are difficult for a long time, we begin to get impatient. Even if there is no apparent solution, we want to grab the bull by the horns and do something about it…anything!

When things are hard, we also tend to wonder if God is really there. It seems to us that this is the ideal time for God to intervene and do something spectacular. After all, that will prove he cares and is concerned, right?

You would have expected Jesus to reason that way. After all, he had been isolated and hungry on the back side of the Judean wilderness for weeks,

all the while acting in service to God. At such a point of physical weakness, it would be so easy to impatiently expect God to provide miraculous protection.

But that wasn't the right way to handle things. Jesus knew that God lovingly provides and protects, without us having to force his hand to do so. So, Jesus, even in the midst of severe temptation, chose to actively trust that "Father knows best." That is one of life's most valuable lessons.

Doesn't it seem strange that we should not test God? After all, isn't he testing us on a continuous basis? Yes, but there is a big difference! The proper purpose of testing is to evaluate against the standard of perfection and to assess the need for improvement. However, since God is perfect in every way, there is absolutely nothing to be gained from any kind of testing. We, on the other hand, have a long way to go. Rarely is that seen more clearly than when we face trials or temptation.

Lord,
Forgive me for impatiently doubting and testing you. I admit that I do not enjoy you testing me. But I thank you that the outcome is to purify my life like spiritual gold.
Amen

The Hope Exchange

If anyone has a right to teach about patience in suffering, it's Jesus. Who else can completely empathize with our pain, disappointment, grief, and loss?

Now he was teaching in one of the synagogues on the sabbath. And just then there appeared a woman with a spirit that had crippled her for eighteen years.

Luke 13:10–11

Over 25 years ago, John Perkins was nearly beaten to death in a Mississippi jail for leading protest marches and boycotts against discrimination. He watched as his children bravely survived the loneliness, cruelty, and emotional stress that accompanied integrating an all-white school in the 1960s.

Like many other African-American leaders during those years, he patiently suffered in many ways to change a nation for the sake of its children. But did those changes and achievements satisfy his—and other civil rights leaders'—longings for community, equality, justice, and peace? I doubt it. As long as violence, hopelessness, inequality, and prejudice exist, we all will suffer.

Does suffering serve a purpose? Definitely! Maybe? I don't know! Why did the woman in Luke 13 have to suffer 18 years before she was healed by Jesus? Again, I don't know.

But I do know that the power of Jesus is greater than any social, physical, emotional, or spiritual ailments experienced by this woman . . . or by us! He offers us hope in exchange for our perseverance.

Just read 2 Corinthians 5:1–10. The Apostle Paul says that we may experience suffering in our earthly bodies, but because of Christ we can look forward to a new home, life, and body in heaven. Let us look to our great Empathizer for hope and endurance because he has patiently suffered for us.

Divine Healer,
When I feel broken, I don't always believe there can be relief. I often don't even think to ask you for help. But you have promised your help, your love, and your comfort. Lord, let me always remember your healing presence.
Amen

Compassion: Your True Vocation

Though we focus on the prodigal son, the story told by Jesus calls us to become like the father, to grow in maturity and to develop a patient watchfulness and a compassionate heart.

So he set off and went to his father. But while he was still far off, his father saw him and was filled with compassion; he ran and put his arms around him and kissed him.

Luke 15:20

The story of the prodigal son is one of the best-known and best-loved stories of the Bible. It has wonderful characters with whom we identify: the rebellious and adventuresome younger son; the hard-working, resentful older brother; the caring, patient, loving father. It has plot twists and humor, like who would have expected a good Jewish boy to be working at a pig farm? It has an unexpected and "feel good" reconciliation as well as a haunting question about whether the older son will join the party. It is a story we can hear again and again. Though the parable is known as the prodigal son, it is equally a story about the patient, loving compassion of the father. Prodigal means "recklessly wasteful or extravagant." We have a prodigal father who is extravagant and lavish with his love.

The late Henri Nouwen, Roman Catholic priest, author, and teacher, once wrote a book called *The Return of the Prodigal Son*. He recounts how in his life he has identified mostly with the younger boy and sometimes with the older son. He was stuck identifying with those two until a friend said to him, "Whether you are the younger son or the elder son, you have to realize that you are called to become the father.... We need you to be a father who can claim for himself the authority of true compassion."

As I have grown older, I see the wisdom in what Nouwen has written. Our true vocation lies in being men and women of compassion, who can feel

Holy God,
Give me a heart of compassion.
Let me see and feel my kinship with
all humanity. Let kindness flow
through my words, blessing abound
in my touch, and gratitude ascend
in my prayers. Touch my heart so I
may love and live as your gracious
son. Thank you, Father.
Amen

another's pain and trust that in that solidarity a healing begins. I find myself less fascinated with the two sons and more drawn to the father.

Sooner or later, it is the father who captures our attention, who draws us to a deeper place of being, who reveals our vocation as a person of compassion. The father is patiently looking for the younger son. He is not anxious or fretting, but seems filled with a prayerful trust that God is watching over the wandering pilgrim. So he watches and waits, willing to let the young adventurer come to his senses. We do not know how long he waited, but he was ever watchful. I want to develop such a patient vigilance in my life. I want that patient

The Return of the Prodigal Son *by Bernardo Licinio*

confidence as I watch my own children make their own journeys of discovery. I need a patient watchfulness because some things cannot be rushed but need the space and time to unfold. Such patient watching is ready, as the prodigal father's was, to respond with welcome and blessing, hugs, and celebrations.

The father also looks with the heart. This is a look of love. Compassion is not a technique mastered or a skill learned. Compassion is the heartfelt solidarity with another. Compassion is an ache in the heart, a longing for another to find their true home.

There is a maturity in the father. He is not concerned about his own needs. His deep faith has ripened into patient compassion.

I am drawn to this mature compassion. I have been torn by labels: young-old, conservative-liberal, activist-contemplative. The father shows a compassionate heart. I want to move beyond the separateness and fear so that I can see everyone on the journey home.

Jesus tells the story to call us home from wherever we have wandered or from whatever resentments have constricted us. Abide in the compassionate love of God that heals, forgives, and renews. Come home and learn to be a person of patient compassion.

"Whether you are the younger son or the elder son, you have to realize that you are called to become the father. . . . You have been looking for friends all your life; you have been craving for affection . . . you have been begging for attention, appreciation and affirmation left and right. The time has come to claim your true vocation—to be a father who can welcome his children home without asking them any questions and without wanting anything from them in return. . . . We need you to be a father who can claim for himself the authority of true compassion."

The Return of the Prodigal Son,
Henri J.M. Nouwen

Rest for the Weary

With all of the stresses and strains of our daily lives, we need Jesus. His love makes life bearable even when things are tough for us. When we take on his yoke and learn his ways, we find rest.

Take my yoke upon you, and learn from me; for I am gentle and humble in heart, and you will find rest for your souls. For my yoke is easy, and my burden is light.

Matthew 11:29–30

"Boy, am I stressed out!" The five-year-old's words seemed incongruous—how could a child be stressed? Or was it simply a repetition of words the child had often heard parents and other adults say in anxious, frustrated voices? We don't have to read the headlines to know that our society is at a high pitch. Many people are barely able to "keep it together," struggling to balance family, work, financial obligations, friendships, personal time. There is much emphasis on time management.

Increased use of computers and other high technology have led to an accelerated pace of life.

So how important it is for us to hear Jesus say, "Come to me, all you that are weary and are carrying heavy burdens, and I will give you rest." Oh, we sigh, filling our lungs with deep breaths, someone understands! There is one who cares when our shoulders ache and our necks are tight with tension. There is one who listens to our inner heartaches and realizes our desire for peace. Jesus invites us to move closer to him, to lean against him, to partake of his strength.

As a carpenter, Jesus surely knew how to fashion a yoke so that it fit the ox well and didn't hurt its neck. And as God's Son, Jesus knew that each of us needs faith that fits us. We have enough burdens that cause anxiety attacks; the burden Jesus shares with us is not heavy but rather is a burden we can manage to carry. When we take Jesus on and put him into our lives, we will find rest for our souls. The stresses and strains of the world around us suddenly take on a new perspective.

All parts of our lives can be seen in the light of the love Jesus has for us. Yes, we may have problems with finances or relationships or jobs, but in the midst of all that is a God who loves us so much. Jesus came to share the load.

Close your eyes and take some deep breaths. Feel the tension in your body. Imagine your to-do list with all its activity and decisions that weigh you down. Then picture Jesus coming toward you. As he nears, he places a yoke on your shoulders.

This is no ordinary yoke. This yoke is feather-light, made of love. Feel Jesus' yoke on your shoulders, and feel the tensions slipping away. Hear him speak your name and say, "Take my yoke upon you, and learn from me; for I am gentle and humble in heart, and you will find rest for your soul. For my yoke is easy, and my burden is light."

Give thanks for this gift and when you are ready, open your eyes, knowing that the yoke of love that lies softly on your shoulders will help you face whatever stresses and strains are part of your life.

Gracious God,
Thank you for Jesus. Help me remember that he is part of my life at all times. He is there in the bad moments and the good, loving me no matter what happens. Sometimes I need a new perspective, God, because in the midst of all I do, I can forget that your love can carry me through. All the rest—the problems, the worries—are temporary, but your love in Jesus Christ is eternal. Let me take this yoke of love that I might serve you always.
Amen

The Transformed and Transforming Cross

The cross was the ultimate symbol of degradation and humiliation, of pain and death, of absolute failure. Through Jesus' passion, death, and resurrection, the cross was transformed into a symbol of limitless love and eventual triumph.

Then Jesus told his disciples, "If any want to become my followers, let them deny themselves and take up their cross and follow me."

Matthew 16:24

The doctor's diagnosis that our newborn son had Down syndrome came as a shock. With four other healthy children, I had assumed that our fifth child would also be fine. That horrible news, which etched my soul, was a life sentence to burdens I could only imagine. I had never even talked to a retarded person! I knew no one who had a handicapped child. How could I ever cope? What about the needs of the rest of the family? What kind of life lay before our son?

For weeks I cried every day. My husband tried to comfort me with the assurance that we'd manage, but his attempts at consolation failed; the burden was too much for me. The open acceptance that the other children gave their youngest brother only emphasized my inadequacies. Whenever I looked at our son, all I saw were the symptoms of Down reflected against the images of future problems. I prayed constantly, though most often the prayer was simply a cry for help. How tragic to regard one's own child as a cross!

One day, God responded to my prayers with a special grace; that grace came as the realization that God did not expect me to perform any miracles! If any miracle was to occur, God would take care of that; God only expected me to do my best, for God knew well both our son's limitations and mine.

Through the support and love of neighbors and friends we managed, with each

Christ Carrying the Cross *by Domenikos T. El Greco*

passing day taking us one step further on our family's life journey. Through the daily caring for our son, I gradually realized that Benjamin really was not that different from our other children; neither was he less human. God had a mission for him in our community and in our family, and together we sought that calling.

As I prayed for courage and openness and perseverance, I learned much through our son. I learned about handicaps and retardation; about learning and teaching; about my own and others' capacity to love; about myself and about God.

Ben is now an adult with many friends and living a very full, productive, joy-filled life. How much I would have missed had he not been born to us—had I not had this wonderful cross to bear. Through him I have encountered other facets of God's love for us, for I now know, in a way beyond words, that God's love is not contingent upon our perfection. As God's children we are all loved.

Our belief in Jesus Christ as the Son of God is based upon the resurrection. In awe we contemplate what our God was willing to endure for us—the passion, death, and resurrection of Jesus. Without the horrors and shame of Good Friday, the emptiness of Saturday, there could be no Easter Sunday. We encounter the reality of the resurrection whenever we experience pain or death. That pain can be transformed, through perseverance and God's grace, into growth, maturity, and even joy and love.

The Door Will Open

Do not give up too easily. Jesus invites us to persist in seeking growth for ourselves and justice for others. Such prayerful, patient persistence does yield fruit.

And he said to them, "Suppose one of you has a friend, and you go to him at midnight and say to him, 'Friend, lend me three loaves of bread; for a friend of mine has arrived, and I have nothing to set before him.' And he answers from within, 'Do not bother me; the door has already been locked, and my children are with me in bed; I cannot get up and give you anything.' I tell you, even though he will not get up and give him anything because he is his friend, at least because of his persistence he will get up and give him whatever he needs."

Luke 11:5–8

Around eleven o'clock, the lights are out in our home and everyone is in bed. A knock on the door at midnight would be very unusual and disturbing, so I know some of the feeling of the friend asleep in this parable of Jesus. Yet Jesus is saying something important about persistence and prayer, and we need to explore the context of the parable so its riches can be tasted.

Travelers in the Middle East would often travel late in the day to miss the scorching heat of midday. There were no air-conditioned cars to make the day more tolerable for travel. In the cooler air of the night there was more activity and travel; it would not be so unusual for a friend to arrive very late.

Gracious hospitality was a sacred obligation to most cultures in the Middle East, and eating was a central part of the practice. For a guest to be fully welcomed, they would need to sit and partake of a meal with the family. The meal formed a friendship connection and no harm could take place during a meal. It would be expected that the homeowner would prepare a feast for the late arriving visitor.

Jesus knocks at the door.

Usually bread was baked fresh each day, enough for that day's needs because preserving foods was difficult in the hot weather. The unexpected guest causes the homeowner to search for bread for the act of hospitality. It would be essential to find bread, and there were no convenience stores around.

Palestinian homes were generally simple one-room homes with the door open during the days and closed at night. The family would huddle

together for warmth in the cool, unheated home. To wake one was to wake the whole household and run the risk of not getting the baby back to sleep.

Jesus says if not for friendship, then at least because of the shameless persistence of the knocker, the sleeper will arise and give the neighbor bread. There are often obstacles in our way of learning a skill or seeking justice that require shameless persistence.

I remember an evening when I was visiting with friends and one of them knew how to juggle. After watching him, I asked him to teach me. He was willing, and I stood next to him and learned one hand of the pattern. I switched sides and learned how it felt using the other hand. Then I had to go put the two halves together. I could throw the three balls up but not catch them; I interrupted a conversation and asked him to show me again. He did, less willingly. I went off to practice again. I was getting closer to catching the balls now. I went to him again and again that

Once to Every Man and Nation

Once to every man and nation
Comes the moment to decide,
In the strife of truth with falsehood,
For the good or evil side;
Some great cause, God's new Messiah,
Offering each the bloom or blight,
And the choice goes by forever
Twixt that darkness and that light.

James Russell Lowell

evening until I could throw and catch the balls in the juggling pattern. I would not give up that evening since I had the teacher there, even if it meant interrupting him several more times and taking myself away from the evening's conversations to learn to juggle.

In order to enjoy the reward of being able to juggle, I had to persist in learning the skill. I had to create a space and time over the next few weeks to patiently practice. I eventually got to a place where I could do more than the basic pattern, and I began to use juggling in my talks and presentations. The smiles of children (and adults) are a fine reward for my patient persistence. Now I often get interrupted, "Will you teach me to juggle?"

In the 1980s, a church in East Berlin felt a strong call to begin prayer meetings for peace and for an end to the divisions in the city that were so clearly symbolized by the Berlin Wall. These Christians persisted in their prayer and in inviting others to join in the prayers for peace. The meetings grew even larger than the one church could hold, so they eventually broadcast the prayer meetings into the courtyard. Their patient persistence in prayer became a groundswell for peace that led to the tearing down of the Berlin Wall.

In learning skills or struggling for justice, prayerful, patient persistence goes a long way to

Consider the postage stamp, my son. It secures success through its ability to stick to one thing till it gets there.
Josh Billings

achieving a goal. If you read Martin Luther King, Jr., or Mahatma Gandhi, you see the advice to persist for justice even in the face of great opposition.

Our growth in faith requires the same kind of patient persistence. We learn to pray by praying. I remember spending time with some Quakers, members of the Society of Friends, who seemed to be comfortable in long periods of silence. I asked them to teach me. "How do you befriend the silence? Teach me to control the distractions in my mind. What do you encounter in the silence?" I spent time with them and persisted in asking questions and practicing. I sat in silence with them and learned from them; the presence of God became more real to me in the silence.

Sometimes we give up too easily. We accept what is as the final word. Acceptance is a wonderful Christian virtue, but so is patient persistence. There are causes worth struggling for, praying for. There are injustices that need to be made right. There are relationships that can be saved. Let us not lose heart but keep on knocking at the door of knowledge, growth, justice, peace, prayer.

Loving God,
Weave courage and
patience together in my life
so that I might be strong in
the face of injustice and
persistent in knocking on
doors. Keep your vision for
me fresh and your hope for
the world alive.
Amen

Justice Will Win Out

Sometimes, it seems like the bad guys always win. Yet God promises that justice will win out in the end. How do we wait patiently until that time?

He said, "In a certain city there was a judge who neither feared God nor had respect for people. In that city there was a widow who kept coming to him and saying, 'Grant me justice against my opponent.' For a while he refused; but later he said to himself, 'Though I have no fear of God and no respect for anyone, yet because this widow keeps bothering me, I will grant her justice, so that she may not wear me out by continually coming.'"

Luke 18:2–5

O ccasionally, we read of a person who was wrongly imprisoned for a crime he did not commit. What did he think about, late at night, lying in his prison cell? Was he angry at those who gave false evidence against him? Bitter about the judge or jury who didn't believe his true story? Resentful of the criminal justice system that, in his case, did injustice?

The judge in this story didn't care about God or the people he was supposed to serve. Justice did not seem to be a priority with him. We wouldn't want to be tried in his court!

Luckily, the judge is only half of the story. We also meet a persistent widow. We don't know the exact cause that she repeatedly brings to the judge. We only know that this widow does not give up. There is something deep in her that wants justice, is determined that justice will win out. In the end, like water wearing away a stone, the woman's efforts pay off and the judge relents. He is just plain tired of her noise.

Justice is truth in action.
Benjamin Disraeli

Jesus wants us to delve deeper into this story, to look at our own lives. Who am I more like—the judge or the widow?

Be Prepared!

The early Christians interpreted the following text as a warning that Christ's Second Coming was imminent. As time passed, this text lost its global immediacy. However, the dramatic personal meaning remains, for the thief in the night, coming we know not when, may be death.

But understand this: if the owner of the house had known in what part of the night the thief was coming, he would have stayed awake and would not have let his house be broken into. Therefore you also must be ready.

Matthew 24:43–44

O ur regard for death is representative of our Christian belief. While death will always have its grieving, its undesirable and sad elements, it is not to be feared as the ultimate evil. If we really believe what we profess, then death is the necessary doorway leading to life everlasting with God.

How do we, as Christians, prepare for the coming of this thief of life? We can start with the practical matters of our death. We make out a will, assuring the wise and just distribution of our assets and liabilities. We can plan our funeral, choosing favorite Scripture readings and music. We can tackle other end-of-life matters also. Such discussions need not be depressing; they concern our reason for being—to be united forever with our Maker.

Attending to these duties is a gift in advance for our loved ones as we now lighten their future burdens. Also, we are assuring them that death will not find us unprepared.

But these tasks reward us even now. Only by confronting the reality of death are we awakened to the reality of life. We focus on relationships—with those around us, with God, assigning love and reconciliation primary place. We appreciate more deeply the joys and beauty of our world. We prioritize our time and talents. Eternity has already begun.

Cynthia has been both my friend and my mentor in faith. When she became terminally ill, I was shocked and railed at God. But Cynthia, characteristically, comforted me. "Do not be sad," she said. "How I look forward to seeing God face-to-face. Finally I shall see my Beloved!"

Ready and Waiting

When was the last time you missed a very important event due to poor planning? Jesus' parable in Matthew 25 reinforces the need for wise preparation and readiness for the special celebrations in our lives.

Ten bridesmaids took their lamps and went to meet the bridegroom. Five of them were foolish, and five were wise. When the foolish took their lamps, they took no oil with them; but the wise took flasks of oil with their lamps. As the bridegroom was delayed, all of them became drowsy and slept.

Matthew 25:1–5

When I moved north to Illinois from Tennessee, I came with the same expectations and anticipation one might have in moving to the Arctic circle. My suitcases were stuffed with boots, wool socks, a parka, mittens, and gloves. Packed away in my car trunk was a winter kit that included flares, a blanket, matches, 50 pounds of salt, and a flashlight.

As a result, when Chicago had one of its worst winters, I was more prepared than most for the mental, physical, and psychological challenges of snow that piled up and wind chills that dropped lower than my outdoor thermometer could measure.

PRAYER HAIKU

Bridegroom is coming
With what do I fill my jar?
Prayers, songs, and praises

While I enjoyed building snowmen and creating snow angels, my neighbors complained constantly about what a fierce winter we were experiencing. The media reported on businesses that lost sales due to the weather. Everyone seemed distressed and unprepared—but me!

Sometimes we perceive those who plan ahead as dull and stodgy. I wonder how the foolish bridesmaids in Matthew 25 would have described the other five who dragged spare oil to a party! I'm guessing their comments were less than kind. Yet it is precisely this diligent preparation that grants us the freedom to be spontaneous and unconstrained.

I want to be just as prepared for future spiritual challenges as I was for my first winter in Chicago. I'll risk being described as a "religious freak" now if it means I'm prepared for Jesus' return. It's better than missing the party altogether!

When Jesus Asks You to Trust

❦

But if God so clothes the grass of the
field, which is alive today and tomorrow is
thrown into the oven, will he not much
more clothe you—you of little faith?

Matthew 6:30

Eternal Commander-in-Chief

In American business, the principle has always been "Start at the bottom and work your way up." Recently, however, there has been a widespread change of attitude to "Start as close to the top as possible." Yet, are we willing to face the huge responsibility that goes with the top positions?

The centurion answered, "Lord, I am not worthy to have you come under my roof; but only speak the word, and my servant will be healed. For I also am a man under authority, with soldiers under me; and I say to one, 'Go,' and he goes, and to another, 'Come,' and he comes, and to my slave, 'Do this,' and the slave does it." When Jesus heard him, he was amazed and said to those who followed him, "Truly I tell you, in no one in Israel have I found such faith."

Matthew 8:8–10

The "chain of command" is a classic military concept that is frequently romanticized. It is exciting to see a courageous commanding officer in the movies or on television make a hard decision that results in a major victory.

But that is only one side of the coin. The chain of command is also a chain of authority. The person in the command structure above is the one with the authority over the next lower level. The lower-ranking soldier must respect that authority and act accordingly.

If this chain of command (and authority) works, the military runs smoothly and efficiently. Unfortunately, if it breaks down, as has happened recently in some high-profile courts-martial, there can be a chaotic outcome. This would, of course, be especially dangerous

if it occurred during wartime.

Obviously, not everyone is willing to operate under authority. Sometimes the problem is that the lower-ranking individual is simply a maverick, unwilling to take orders. Sometimes the person in authority takes advantage of their power position and acts in an immoral way.

More often, the problem has to do with trust. Either the soldier of lower rank does not consider the one holding a higher rank to be trustworthy, or, for whatever reason, simply chooses not to trust in the commands being given. Either reason is clearly detrimental.

There is an amazing parallel here to what is involved in placing our trust in the Lord. The Roman centurion certainly understood the necessity of trust. Those under his authority trusted him as commander and, thus, they acted upon such trust when the order was given. The centurion himself was under authority and was fully ready to trust and obey. Thus, he communicated to Jesus his willingness to completely trust Jesus in regard to the healing of his servant.

The centurion had concluded that Jesus was his rightful spiritual commander and wholly trustworthy. So he trusted Jesus to act in the best interest of those under his authority, as any good commanding military officer would.

Perhaps it is harder to trust today in an atmosphere in which authority is often openly disregarded. Perhaps part of the problem is that so many in authority don't really deserve respect or trust.

That is certainly not the case with Jesus. Because he has proven himself to be completely trustworthy, he cannot be the problem. Rather, the heart of the issue is choosing to trust the Lord and wisely accepting his loving authority over your life.

Lord,
I willingly place myself
under your authority as my
wise Commander. You fully
understand the wider
scope of life, and my
understanding is very
limited. I trust you to do
what is best, whether I
understand it or not.
Amen

Healing Comes Through Faith

When we pray for something specific, we may wonder why God does not instantly grant our request. Things turn out differently than we'd planned; we may doubt that God is really in charge. It may take time—and persistent faith—to realize that God eventually brings good to every situation.

Then suddenly a woman who had been suffering from hemorrhages for twelve years came up behind him and touched the fringe of his cloak; for she said to herself, "If I only touch his cloak, I will be made well." Jesus turned, and seeing her he said, "Take heart, daughter; your faith has made you well." And instantly the woman was made well.

Matthew 9:20–22

64

Courage comes in many forms. For the hemorrhaging woman, the act of reaching out to touch Jesus' cloak was an act of incredible bravery. Here she was, suffering with a condition involving "an issue of blood," and therefore ritually unclean by Jewish law. And there was Jesus on his way to bring a young girl back to life, a holy man surrounded by his disciples and a crowd of people. Did she dare? Would his healing power be enough to stop the flow of blood?

For 12 long years, she had been an outcast because of her illness. In desperation, she had tried every known possible remedy. Was it the news that Jesus was a healer that helped her reach her hand forward to touch the fringe of his garment as he passed? Did she find strength when she saw the look of compassion on his face? Whatever it was that finally guided her to make contact, there

was power in the words Jesus spoke to her. "Your faith has made you well."

All the years of suffering had led to this moment of clarity, when this woman's life was changed by faith in Jesus. Not only was her physical body made new, but we can be sure that her spirit was touched by her connection to Jesus, as well. Her entire future opened up before her, ripe with new possibility.

Can you think of a time in your life when your faith led you to wholeness? Don't

She, too, who touched thee in the press and healing virtue stole,
was answered, "Daughter, go in peace: thy faith hath made thee whole."
Like her, with hopes and fears we come to touch thee if we may;
O send us not despairing home; send none unhealed away.

William Cowper

just focus on times of physical illness. Often, our minds and hearts need healing, too. In 1967, Percy had a falling out with his sister. His long-harbored grudge festered until, giving over the need for revenge to Jesus, he was able to reconnect to his sister and realized a new lightness of heart. His faith made him well. Andrea battled low self-esteem and stage fright that hindered her professionally until a spiritual friend helped her give her life to Jesus. When she realized how much Jesus loved her, she was able to work through her psychological problems: Her faith made her well.

Jesus,
I believe in you.
Your power is real and available to me.
Give me the faith to trust in you,
knowing that if I reach out, you will be
there for me.
In your powerful name I pray,
Amen

Where is the area of your life that could use healing? The power of Jesus is there for us, as it was for the woman who, weary of 12 years of bleeding, reached out for help. Jesus can touch your body, soul, relationships, and work life to heal them—we just need to reach out to the Living Christ and ask for help. Imagine him extending his loving arms toward you and your needs. "Take heart," he says, "your faith has made you well."

Even the Smallest Faith

Believing and acting on your beliefs are important parts of faith. Jesus commends us for what seem like small acts or humble words. God transforms what we offer into hope for the world.

If you have faith the size of a mustard seed, you will say to this mountain, "Move from here to there," and it will move; and nothing will be impossible for you.

Matthew 17:20

When my children were very young, one of their favorite books was *The Little Engine That Could*. It was the story of a small train engine that admired all the big locomotive engines in the train yard but never got asked to do any significant work. I don't remember the reason, but one day it gets asked to take a train of goodies for boys and girls up a big hill. The words it says as it huffs and puffs up the hill are, "I think I can, I think I can, I think I can." Over and over, the little engine repeats the chant until it succeeds in cresting the hill and then descends to a cheering crowd of boys and girls—with my children cheering, too.

"I think I can, I think I can" was one of the first notions of faith for my children. Size was not the important ingredient, but belief and desire. When my children read the story of little David and the giant Goliath in the Bible, they learned again that size was not the key; it was David's belief that God was with him and his knowledge that he was very good with a slingshot.

Faith does not have to be grand, complete, big, or perfect. Faith is the willingness to believe, to trust that something can happen, so we give ourselves over to the effort. Faith for the Christian is the willingness to step out in confidence that there is a God. Faith is believing that God cares about us and is with us in all our efforts.

Jesus is encouraging the disciples to have faith, to trust a little deeper, to have the confidence that with God all things are possible. He uses two images that would be familiar to his listeners. Though mustard seeds are not the smallest seeds, it was common to use them as an illustration of smallness. Jesus is encouraging the disciples' belief and confidence in this way. Keep trusting. Keep loving. Keep praying. You don't have to have it all figured out. Take one more step. A small step even.

Recall a time your small effort played a part in a grand result. Give thanks to God for people whose words and deeds influenced you for the good. Put a mustard seed in a small container that you will see often—use it as a call to prayer.

In Hebrew circles, great teachers would often use the image of moving mountains as a way of encouraging listeners to overcome difficulties. Jesus chooses this second image, moving mountains, to point out to and encourage the disciples that the hardest tasks of life can be accomplished with the smallest of faith. What seems insurmountable and impossible, mountain-big, can be overcome by even a little faith.

I am touched by all the things that happen because of one word or one act. Something that seems insignificant can make a huge difference. One visit to a worship service can start a person on the journey of faith. One teacher can make the difference for a student. One mountain-top experience or religious revival can call a person to a new vocation. One senseless tragedy can spur a community to open a teen center. One candle lit in the darkness can chase away the dark.

One afternoon, I mentioned to a church member that I wondered if she would be interested in creating a time and space at church where a storyteller could come to perform. She jumped at the idea and has birthed a program of bringing storytellers who attract new people to the church. One small idea met with the faith of one person who created the program.

In December 1955, Rosa Parks was tired from working all day and was glad for a seat on the bus going home. When some white people got on the bus, Rosa was asked to move to the back with the rest of the blacks. She refused, and her arrest motivated the blacks in Montgomery, Alabama, to call for a bus boycott. The person chosen to lead the boycott was a young pastor named Martin Luther King, Jr. One person's small act can catalyze a new "I think I can" movement for social change.

God can take our smallest acts, our seemingly insignificant words, and use them for good. We can turn our best efforts over to God and trust that they fit into God's plan for justice and peace, healing and unity upon the earth.

Faith Finds a Way

Some people view obstacles as dead ends. Others conclude that those same obstacles are merely cleverly disguised opportunities. What makes the difference between these opposite outlooks?

Then some people came, bringing to him a paralyzed man, carried by four of them. And when they could not bring him to Jesus because of the crowd, they removed the roof above him; and after having dug through it, they let down the mat on which the paralytic lay. When Jesus saw their faith, he said to the paralytic, "Son, your sins are forgiven."

Mark 2:3–5

Conventional wisdom says, "Where there's a will, there's a way." But spiritual wisdom, the kind of wisdom that comes from Jesus, takes an extra, necessary step. Where's there's a will, there's the ability to choose to trust. And where there's trust in the Lord, there's a way!

A classic example of this kind of faith was seen when four people brought a paralyzed man to Jesus to be healed. The crowd that had come to see Jesus was so thick that the people with the paralytic couldn't get into the building where Jesus was. The huge crowd would have been enough to convince most people to give up and go home.

But these four were not most people. They firmly believed Jesus

could heal their paralyzed loved one, and they were determined to find a way to get him to Jesus.

Still, there was no way in through the conventional entrances. But why limit the options to conventional ones? These men of faith decided to go up the outside stairs and open a hole in the flat tile or clay roof of the building. Through the opening, they lowered down the paralytic directly into the presence of Jesus.

Lord,
We know that if life were
smooth sailing, there would
be no need for faith. We thank
you for the opportunity to
trust you tenaciously, in spite
of the obstacles in our paths.
Amen

Almost anyone else would have been shocked at the nerve of this plan to crash the party, right through the roof. Jesus, instead, was moved by the faith that motivated this extraordinarily creative approach. He did not scold the invaders. He commended them for their faith and extended the eternal gift of forgiveness.

Almost everyone encounters obstacles in their lives on a fairly consistent basis. The real question is, "Do you see them as insurmountable obstacles or challenging opportunities?"

Gratefulness Begins in the Heart

Have you ever cut open a delicious-looking piece of fruit only to discover it was almost completely rotten inside? How disappointing! Perhaps God feels much the same way when we focus more on our outer behavior than on our inner motives.

Then Jesus asked, "Were not ten made clean? But the other nine, where are they? Was none of them found to return and give praise to God except this foreigner?" Then he said to him, "Get up and go on your way; your faith has made you well."

Luke 17:17–19

After being married for over 20 years, my husband, Stan, and I have settled into a ritual-type approach to sharing household chores. He takes out the garbage, runs the dishwasher, mows the lawn, shovels the snow, vacuums, and tends to our Sheltie's pressing needs in the early morning hours. I'm responsible for cooking, laundry, plant care, paying bills, toilets, and nighttime dog duty.

Our approach works pretty well, but every once in a while, I get home from work to discover that Stan has prepared dinner or a load of much needed laundry has been done or the dog has already had her walk. On other occasions when I see Stan is tired or busy, I've been  known to run the dishwasher, vacuum up the dog hair that coats our floor, and gather the recyclables for pick-up.

We stick with our household assignments most of the time, but whenever one of us makes the effort to go beyond what is expected, the effect is significant.

Luke tells the story of ten lepers who appealed to Jesus for healing. Jesus instructed them to show themselves to a priest for purification. As the ten began their journey, they were healed. Nine continued on their way. Only one turned back to say thanks, and he wasn't even a Jew! As the foreigner threw himself at Jesus' feet, Jesus posed the three questions found in Luke 17:17–19.

"Were not ten made clean?" Jesus already knew the answer. He had healed them.

"But the other nine, where are they?" He already knew the answer to this question as well. The nine were seeing the priest as Jesus had instructed.

"Was none of them found to return and give praise to God except this foreigner?" Again, Jesus already knew that the Samaritan was the only one who had returned.

For the Beauty of the Earth

For the beauty of the earth,
For the glory of the skies,
For the love which from our birth
Over and around us lies;
Lord of all, to Thee we raise
This our hymn of grateful praise.

For Thyself, best gift divine,
To our race so freely given;
For that great, great love of Thine,
Peace on earth and joy in heaven:
Lord of all, to Thee we raise
This our hymn of grateful praise.

Folliott S. Pierpoint, altered

What right did Jesus have to question the motives of the nine lepers? Weren't they following his precise instructions? So why was he so upset that only one came back? If I had been one of the nine, I would probably have responded with, "Hey, I'm doing exactly what you told me to do. I'm being completely obedient."

If we do exactly what Jesus tells us to do, doesn't that guarantee that he will be pleased with us? I used to think so, but I don't think this story bears out my assumption.

Pleasing Jesus is not just a matter of obedience, just as pleasing my husband is not just a matter of doing what he expects or what we have agreed upon in our marriage. Faithfulness and gratitude begin internally with our attitudes. Too often we point to our generous actions and behavior while muttering and complaining in our hearts.

If we begin to focus more on our outward actions, neglecting the nurture of Christlike attitudes, we face the possibility of developing legalistic rituals. While Stan and I expect each other to follow through on the chores we've committed to be responsible for, the extra touches of helping, being sensitive, and building each other up must not be ignored. Filling my car up with gas without being asked, making a run to the store, giving me a back rub when he's the tired one—these are all acts that reflect Stan's inner attitude toward me. My heart, in return, is filled with appreciation, love, and thankfulness that I have a spouse who is willing to go these extra miles.

In the same way, Jesus expects our hearts to be filled with appreciation, love, and thankfulness for all he has done for us. What acts of praise, surrender, worship, and thanks have you offered him lately? Remember, Jesus says this kind of grateful faith brings healing.

Lord, Let Me See

Some people are unable to see because of damage to or a defect in their eyes. Others, however, choose not to see, succumbing to egotism or self-righteousness, materialism or prejudice, greed or fear, love of power or even self-hate. Whatever the cause, blindness can result.

Jesus stood still and ordered the man to be brought to him; and when he came near, he asked him, "What do you want me to do for you?" He said, "Lord, let me see again." Jesus said to him, "Receive your sight; your faith has saved you." Immediately he regained his sight and followed him, glorifying God; and all the people, when they saw it, praised God.

Luke 18:40–43

The hero of this story, being physically blind, was unable to see the cause of the commotion and questioned those around him. "Jesus of Nazareth is passing by," he was informed. The blind man, recognizing Jesus as the Christ, the Anointed One, the Son of David, added his voice to the crowd. And Jesus stopped in his journey.

Jesus heals the blind man.

Was it the man's shouting or the man's believing that brought the journey to a halt? Did Jesus pause in his travels because of the presence of the crowd or the presence of such great faith? In the direct encounter between the two men, Jesus asked the man what he wanted, for clearly the man already possessed the ability to see beyond the physical to the spiritual reality. When he asked for his sight, Jesus, the Divine Physician, granted his request. Having his physical sight allowed the man to carry out what his faith had prepared him for—to follow Jesus.

I believe Lord,
help my unbelief!
With the trust of that Spirit-filled man
I ask for healing and sight.
With the faith of the healed one,
I follow you,
Son of God.

Be Worthy of God's Trust

God gives us life and trusts that we will live it well. If we use the gifts God has given us, we will be rewarded and see positive results for our efforts.

So he said, "A nobleman went to a distant country
to get royal power for himself and then return.
He summoned ten of his slaves, and gave them
ten pounds, and said to them, 'Do business with
these until I come back.' But the citizens of his
country hated him and sent a delegation after him,
saying, 'We do not want this man to rule over us.'
When he returned, having received royal power,
he ordered these slaves, to whom he had given
the money, to be summoned so that he might find
out what they had gained by trading. The first came
forward and said, 'Lord, your pound has made

*ten more pounds.' He said to him, 'Well done,
good slave! Because you have been trustworthy
in a very small thing, take charge of ten cities.'"*

Luke 19:12–17

When someone was needed to run a weekly tutoring program for elementary children, Nicole applied for the volunteer position. She was only a high school junior and had never had this much responsibility, but she loved children and hoped one day to be a teacher. Nicole was thrilled to be given the job; she threw herself into her work, amazed that the school would trust her with the program. Nicole spent time getting to know the younger kids and their needs. She assessed the tutors, figuring out their strengths so she could team up young elementary students needing help in math and reading with high school students who wanted to help.

As she worked with the tutoring program, Nicole took on more responsibilities. She began to see herself as a teacher and found her own

Work is love made visible.
        Kahlil Gibran

strengths in assessing learning needs and coordinating the program. When she received a community service award, Nicole was proud of what she had accomplished. In her acceptance speech, she noted, "As a teenager, it felt great to be trusted and then to be able to prove my trustworthiness. This experience has helped me know my own capabilities."

Nicole realized what the slave in our parable discovered when his master gave him one pound to use, instructed only to "Do business with [this] until I come back." The first slave was able to come forward when the nobleman returned and say, "Lord, your pound has made ten more pounds." It pleased the master to know that this slave had made good use of his money, so he rewarded the first slave with more responsibility "because you have been trustworthy in a very small thing."

It feels great to deserve another's trust. When someone gives us a job, assumes we can

handle the tasks at hand, or wants our input, we get the message: We are valued. God, in giving us not only our very life but the freedom to make our own choices, trusts our spirits as well as our capabilities.

Look at your life. How have you proved trustworthy to God? What actions have you taken that best respond to a loving Creator who wants to count on you as a faithful servant? Have you felt rewarded for a life well lived? Hear God say to you, "Well done!"

This is a time to also admit the instances when you may not have fulfilled God's expectations. Were you more like the

I am no longer my own, but thine.
Put me to what thou wilt,
rank me with whom thou wilt…
Let me be full, let me be empty.
Let me have all things, let me have nothing.
I freely and heartily yield all things
to thy pleasure and disposal…
thou art mine, and I am thine…

John Wesley

other slave (see Luke 19:20–22) who did nothing with the money, fearing what the master might do? Do you have gifts and talents you have been reluctant to use for God's service? Let this parable open a door in your heart so that you might be bold in living a trustworthy life.

Water, Wind, and Faith

Jesus challenges us to have faith in God even in the midst of the windstorms of our lives.

✦

*A windstorm arose on the sea, so great that the boat
was being swamped by the waves; but he was
asleep. And they went and woke him up, saying,
"Lord, save us! We are perishing!" And he said to
them, "Why are you afraid, you of little faith?"
Then he got up and rebuked the winds and
the sea; and there was a dead calm.*

Matthew 8:24–26

✦

Even when there is no water around, we know what it is like to be in that boat. We even use similar language. We have "stormy" days, "stormy" relationships. We are "swamped" by all the work we have to do. We feel the list growing of things to do. We see the

approaching deadlines. We know the pressure to achieve much and accomplish more. When we add the family calendar, the relatives, and the needs of the world, our boat often seems ready to capsize.

"But he was asleep." Sometimes it feels like there is no way out. The problems threaten to dump us into the sea, and we cannot see how we are going to make it.

At such times we cry out, "Help!" We want Jesus, or someone, to save us. Scripture is full of such cries. "Save me, O God, for the waters have come up to my neck" (Psalm 69:1). We are in good company when we cry out to God.

Our challenge is to trust that not only does God hear our cry, but that he is also working in the very midst of our windstorm. Jesus is revealing to the disciples and to us a God who cares for the well-being of all people, especially those feeling swamped.

We need not worry how God will calm the storms, only that he will. Each storm calmed leads us to greater trust, a deeper faith. God can help us deal with the constant pressures of our days. God can bring calm to our stormy lives.

At its core, faith is not a system of knowledge, but trust.

Joseph Ratzinger

Can It!

An educational campaign has been running an ad where mothers are asked, "What's the worst four-letter word your child can say?" The moms respond, "Can't." We can overcome self-doubt and become high achievers.

***

So Peter got out of the boat, started walking on the water, and came toward Jesus. But when he noticed the strong wind, he became frightened, and beginning to sink, he cried out, "Lord, save me!" Jesus immediately reached out his hand and caught him, saying to him, "You of little faith, why did you doubt?"

Matthew 14:29–31

***

Peter saw Jesus walking on water, and he decided to try it, too. After he took a few steps, it's as if he realized, "Hey, I can't do this." He began to sink, and Jesus had to help him. But it seems to me that Jesus was chiding the wrong person. If I had been Peter, I would have said, "But Lord, at least I got out of the boat! Matthew and Thaddeus are still in the boat!"

Perhaps Peter knew that Jesus was holding him to a higher standard. After all, Peter had that glimmer of "can" in his eyes. That's what made it so tragic when his thinking shifted to "can't"!

By nature, I'm something of a can't thinker. You want me to try the new roller coaster at the amusement park? Can't do it. Tell my boss what I really think? Can't.

The Calling of St. Peter *by Hans Suss Von Kulbach*

Jesus,
Even though I've never been as confident as The Little Engine That Could, *help me to shift my thinking in the future to "I know* **you** *can. I know* **you** *can."*
Amen

I'm becoming aware of things I can't do. What I'm trying to learn is that even if I (or Peter or you) can't, we need to let Jesus show us that he can. It's no big deal to miss the experience of an amusement ride. But the spiritual consequences of Can't Syndrome are more significant. How many relationships do I miss by saying can't? How many bold new adventures?

I'm not sure Jesus rebukes our doubt because he's hurt by it; I think it's because he knows what we will miss!

Facing the Storm

Whatever storms we face, Jesus has the power to calm our fears if we recognize him and allow him to take charge of our lives.

❧❧❧

He woke up and rebuked the wind, and said to the sea, "Peace! Be still!" Then the wind ceased, and there was a dead calm. He said to them, "Why are you afraid? Have you still no faith?" And they were filled with great awe and said to one another, "Who then is this, that even the wind and the sea obey him?"

Mark 4:39–41

❧❧❧

Jesus was asleep when the storm began. As the wind stirred up the waves on the Sea of Galilee, the others became more and more afraid, realizing that this voyage could be their last if the boat capsized or sank.

Terrified, they awoke their teacher. He rebuked the storm and the wind ceased, leaving only the shining calm of the lake's surface under and around the boat. Jesus must have seen something on his followers' faces that showed that their fear was not assuaged. "Why are you afraid?" he asked. "Have you still no faith?" It was then that the truth sank in: Jesus had calmed the storm. "Who then is this," they cried, "that even the wind and sea obey him?"

All along, there had been some who followed Jesus only to see the miracles. He may have been for them a worker of magic, the best show in town. They may have been attracted by

Jesus calms the storm.

his storytelling, intrigued by his teachings. Now his power had been revealed. This was no sideshow magician; he could calm storms.

Perhaps it was then that all Jesus had ever said began to make sense. Now, on a boat out at sea, some of Jesus' followers realized that this powerful man was one to whom they could commit their lives. Little did they know that 2,000 years later, Jesus would still be calming the fears and stormy lives of his followers. The storms we face may not be wind and water but the turbulence of our lives. Jesus can calm our storms.

Loving Jesus,
We need you. Our boat is small
and the sea is large, and we
are sometimes afraid. Be with
us as we remember that in you
is our salvation.
Amen

An Invitation to Believe

Jesus wants to move us from unbelief to belief. He invites us to trust God, beginning with the simple, ordinary moments of life.

He answered them, "You faithless generation, how much longer must I be among you? How much longer must I put up with you? Bring him to me." And they brought the boy to him. When the spirit saw him, immediately it convulsed the boy.... Jesus asked the father, "How long has this been happening to him?" And he said, "From childhood. It has often cast him into the fire and into the water, to destroy him; but if you are able to do anything, have pity on us and help us." Jesus said to him, "If you are able!— All things can be done for the one who believes." Immediately the father of the child cried out, "I believe; help my unbelief!"

Mark 9:19–24

When I was in high school, I played doubles on the tennis team. It was a lesson in trust and faith as well as a lot of fun. I had to have faith that my partner would get the balls that were hit on his side of the court, and that he would be able to win his serve or get the next point (especially if I had just made an error). This faith was based on experience, on past games when he had come through. This faith enabled me to do my part

and not run on his side of the court whenever a ball was hit to him. Faith in my partner and faith in myself led to a way of playing; it was a commitment based on faith.

Jesus is lamenting the lack of faith in the disciples, the

crowd, and the father. Such a lack of faith is paralyzing, and when Jesus arrives on the scene, he learns that the disciples have not been able to help the boy. A whole world of disbelief dwelt in that crowd and stood in the way of healing.

Our generation may not be much different; we too often doubt the power of God to work in our contemporary situations. Sometimes we feel that the international problems, the violence in the cities, the growing numbers of homeless, and the lack of support for education are beyond the realm of solutions. We often don't believe that God can figure out how to solve the mess we have gotten ourselves into.

Jesus knows how hard it is to have faith in these trying times. We are a mixture of belief and unbelief. We believe there is a God, yet we are timid in

O for a Thousand Tongues to Sing

O for a thousand tongues to sing my great Redeemer's praise,
the glories of my God and King, the triumph of his grace!
My gracious Master and my God, assist me to proclaim,
to spread thro' all the earth abroad the honors of your name.

Charles Wesley

believing that God can bring about healing or world peace. We see evidence of God in the wonders of creation, yet we find it difficult to see how God is at work in our hurt and pain. Jesus wants us to deepen our trust in God. He wants us to come to God sooner with our requests and needs. He wants us to know that God desires to help us and is able to help us.

Such faith is a gift. We do not earn God's help. It is offered before we are even aware that we have needs. We simply turn and receive. We let go and let God. Faith is not some system of knowledge that we have to master, rather it is a way of trusting. Faith is not a set of propositions to believe but a way of living with what small measure of confidence in God that we have. We start small, perhaps thanking God for the gift of a new day. We look around at creation and let a prayer of thanks arise. Start with one rose, one sunrise and say, "Thank you."

A friend of mine came to church one Sunday to help honor the nursery school teachers who teach his children. He had missed the services we had done previous years, but on this Sunday, he decided to come. He says he felt so safe in the sanctuary that he cried through much of the service. The tears were the beginning of his faith. It was a small thing to come to church, and he did not understand what the tears meant, but it was the beginning of turning himself over to God. He has hardly missed a Sunday since, and then he started coming to some classes and dropping by the office during the week.

Faith is not simply a content to be learned but a commitment to be lived.

Robert McAfee Brown

Each day, he was learning to trust God more. The day of his baptism was a glorious day, and he is daily moving from unbelief to belief.

We learn over and over to trust God. Each day is a new chance to deepen our trust. I have been helped in the daily trust of God by thinking about each breath that I take. The air we breathe is the same air that Jesus breathed. We are filled with the breath of God every time we breathe. God is in me and all around me. I hope each day to be more aware of this wonder. Take a few moments to focus on your breathing, and give thanks to God for this gift.

The Good Shepherd

Faith grows as we admit our doubts. Is this not what the father in this gospel story did? He knew he didn't have complete faith, but he offered what he had for the sake of his son. We can be honest with God about our doubts. We can offer them for God's healing, liberating touch. Each day is a day to move from unbelief to belief.

We know more faith is demanded of us so it helps if we can connect ourselves to the community of faith. The church can help us in our struggle. We hear the stories of how others live out their faith. We ask for prayers. We sing the great hymns of tradition, songs of faith that through the wonder of music and lyric plant their stories in us. We challenge and console one another as we describe our journeys and reflect on our faithfulness. We laugh and cry together and know that God wants to move us from lament to praise. Praise God.

Faith is a firm and certain knowledge of God's benevolence toward us, founded upon the truth of the freely given promise in Christ, both revealed to our minds and sealed upon our hearts through the Holy Spirit.

John Calvin

Have Faith in God

No matter what stage of life we're at, God can use us for good in the world. With open hearts, our lives can bear fruit even if our bodies are no longer youthful or strong. Faith in God keeps us focused on what really matters: bearing fruit as followers of Jesus.

In the morning as they passed by, they saw the fig tree withered away to its roots. Then Peter remembered and said to him, "Rabbi, look! The fig tree that you cursed has withered." Jesus answered them, "Have faith in God."

Mark 11:20–22

By the time I met Merry Harter, she was already in her seventies, at least. Her pastor called me and said, "One of my members has moved to your neck of the woods. Why don't you go over to visit her in the nursing home?" I'm ashamed to admit that my first response was, wearily, "Another old person to visit." Was I ever in for an education!

I visited Merry when she had only been at the nursing home for a short time. In her inimitable way, however, she had already organized a weekly Bible study, a monthly worship service, and had signed up to tutor ESL (English as a Second Language) elementary students with reading.

Despite the fact that her swollen knees made walking difficult, Merry seemed to be constantly on the go. I may have expected her energy to be "withered" by age, but I was wrong. Merry was a go-getter with an inner energy that came from her deep faith in God.

If wrinkles must be written upon our brows, let them not be written upon the heart. The spirit should never grow old.

James A. Garfield

Merry never let herself become depressed because of physical pain or her inability to be active. (When she retired from her nursing career, she volunteered for the Peace Corps in Tanzania!) Out of her deep life of prayer, she focused on what she could still do even when walking was difficult. Faith in God kept Merry's spirit strong even as her body began to wear down with age and infirmity. What an example to us all!

Faith-Sticking

One of my favorite bits on a current cartoon is when the children keep asking the father for something, and he keeps saying no. But their unrelenting persistence in asking the same question over and over wears him down and he finally shrieks, "OK!" Oddly enough, Jesus tells us this should be the tactic we use in asking for God's help.

And will not God grant justice to his chosen ones who cry to him day and night? Will he delay long in helping them? I tell you, he will quickly grant justice to them. And yet, when the Son of Man comes, will he find faith on earth?

Luke 18:7–8

I don't know about you, but more than once I've cried to God day and night. I am definitely a crier! When my best friend's daughter was born with a genetic disorder that claimed her life within days, I cried to God. As I watched the news coverage of the Oklahoma bombing in 1995, I cried to

God for justice. When I saw the devastation of the 1997 flooding in North Dakota, I pleaded with God for help. And when close family members started talking about divorce, I couldn't help crying for guidance, forgiveness, and mercy.

I wonder why God has allowed such devastating events to rock my—and others'—faith. Sometimes, on the surface, it seems easier to be faithful when our lives are free from pain and chaos. But perhaps this is only cheap faith.

Evidence and models of faithfulness in difficult times seem rare these days. Not often do we see tenacious faith like that of the woman in Luke 18. In these two verses, Jesus is commenting on a parable where a beleaguered widow used the cartoon tactic to demand justice from a reluctant judge. Jesus is not saying that God represents a self-centered (uncaring?) judge. But I think what he's trying to tell us is that sometimes we believe God has told us "no," when in reality his answer is "not yet." Consequently, we give up too soon and miss out on the opportunities and blessings of a persistent faith.

Perhaps we give up because we've had unpleasant experiences in the past where our enthusiasm to convince a parent backfired. We learned that if we went past a certain point, we would likely hear, "I said *no,* and I MEAN NO!"

As a result, we stopped asking for our needs to be met. We stopped getting our hopes up. We determined that we would rather do without than get yelled at. Then we grew up, became adults, and now assume God will

snap at us just as our parents did.

Let's consider why a good parent might deny a child's request. I can think of several:

Timing—Saying yes to candy right before dinner can ruin an appetite.

Safety—A six year old may want to drive, swim alone, or use the chain saw, but a wise parent won't allow it.

Degree—A parent might say no to a teenager's request for a junker in order to buy a better, more reliable car. Or conversely, a parent might say no to the request for a sports car and buy a sedan instead.

Discipline—Stopping at the neighborhood water park on your way to a week's vacation at the beach may be short-sighted and prevent a child from experiencing the rewards of patience. Immediately saying yes to every request also gives children the impression that parents are at their beck and call.

Might not these same reasons apply to our requests or cries to God? Just as parents love, guide, and protect their children because they understand the big picture, God loves, guides, and protects us because he has an eternal perspective. Our wisdom is limited. I have to believe an infinitely wise God might know more than I do about long-term consequences and options.

I Have Decided to Follow Jesus

I have decided to follow Jesus,
I have decided to follow Jesus,
I have decided to follow Jesus,
No turning back, no turning back.

Tho' none go with me, I still will follow,
Tho' none go with me, I still will follow,
Tho' none go with me, I still will follow,
No turning back, no turning back.

The world behind me, the cross before me;
The world behind me, the cross before me;
The world behind me, the cross before me;
No turning back, no turning back.

Will you decide now to follow Jesus?
Will you decide now to follow Jesus?
Will you decide now to follow Jesus?
No turning back, no turning back.

Source unknown

But while I wait for clear signals from God, Jesus actually encourages me to "cry out to him day and night." Sometimes it's not easy to keep asking for the same thing when I keep hearing no—or when I don't hear anything at all.

When my friend's infant daughter died, I grieved over God's no. But when her twin boys were born 14 months later, I rejoiced at God's answer. As I watched the news coverage of the Oklahoma bombing trial, I was reminded of God's justice. When I read of the contributions and help provided to those who lost so much in the floods in Fargo, I thanked God for working through his people. As the dissension continues in my own family, I am still waiting to hear God's answer.

Yet, maybe that's what faith is all about. If I only give God the same amount of time, effort, energy, or deadlines I give any other person, that's not much faith on my part. Maybe that's another reason why faith seems so rare these days. We accumulate misperceptions and faults from parents, bosses, friends, siblings, and others, and then we assume we will get the same response from God.

I believe (at least try to) that if I keep asking, God will eventually answer. I want to stick it out long enough to hear him.

Failure: A Detour to Success

It has been observed that the only people who don't fail very much are those who don't try very much. Does that point also hold true with faith?

Simon, Simon, listen! Satan has demanded to sift all of you like wheat, but I have prayed for you that your own faith may not fail; and you, when once you have turned back, strengthen your brothers.

Luke 22:31–32

I f Simon Peter had been in the military, he would have been one of the most decorated veterans in history. He showed great courage in some very difficult situations. Often the courage grew out of faith, such as when he walked on water. But the danger of a serious "blowout" in his faith existed. For example, after he had walked on water for a distance, he began to sink. Jesus made it clear that the problem was a momentary failure of faith. That doubt was a dangerous chink in Peter's spiritual armor.

For all his great acts of courage, however, there was one instance in which Peter was a world-class failure. And make no mistake about it. It was, without argument, a failure of faith.

Simon had been at the top of the class among Jesus' prize pupils. And not only was he a quick study, he was the natural leader among the apostles. He had even been given the affectionate nickname Peter (meaning "Rock" or "Rocky") by Jesus, implying a key foundational role Simon would play in the church in the time ahead. Yes, things were going very well as long as they were headed in the direction that Peter thought they should go.

Unfortunately, that didn't continue. Jesus eventually had to tell his closest followers what was on the horizon for him on their trip to Jerusalem. In keeping with God's plan, Jesus would have to suffer at the hands of the Jewish authorities and be sentenced to die on a Roman cross, before being raised from the dead.

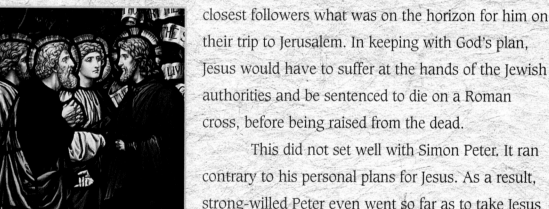

Jesus greets Peter and the other disciples.

This did not set well with Simon Peter. It ran contrary to his personal plans for Jesus. As a result, strong-willed Peter even went so far as to take Jesus aside and rebuke him. This was the first time Jesus had to warn Peter that he was unconsciously playing into Satan's hands with such short-sighted thinking.

What a shock that must have been to Peter! To be told by the Master that the Devil was using your deep concern would be highly confusing, to say the least. Perhaps it was even a little disillusioning, sowing a small seed of doubt in Peter's mind.

Then, after Jesus and the apostles arrived in Jerusalem, the warning was repeated, and at a very ironic point. The issue came up immediately after Jesus had spoken of the faithfulness of the apostles in trials. He promised them close fellowship and the authority to rule under him in the coming kingdom of God.

So far, so good! This was indeed music to Peter's ears. But Jesus then struck a sour note. He brought up Satan's eagerness to sift the lives of the apostles like so many kernels of grain. Most troubling of all was that Jesus focused this point at Simon Peter. Jesus pointed his finger at Peter, clearly implying that, although Satan desired to trouble the lives of all the apostles, he was particularly intent on getting to Peter.

But Jesus didn't stop there. Although he knew there would be a short-term failure of faith on the part of Peter and the other apostles, Jesus would

not allow it to be long-term or permanent. He had prayed to the Father to enable Peter to get beyond that painful failure and to help restore and build up others in the Lord.

Jesus saw it coming, and he once again alerted Peter to the grave danger. But Peter wouldn't listen. He objected to Jesus' assertion, this time indicating that he had at least heard what Jesus had previously taught about his coming mistreatment and death in Jerusalem. He pledged allegiance to Jesus, no matter what might happen. He claimed to be willing to go to prison for Jesus, or even to die.

But Jesus knew that would not happen, at least not immediately (though Peter was imprisoned more than once and died for Jesus later in his career). So Jesus indicated just how close at hand the danger to his faith was. Simon Peter would deny even knowing Jesus three times before the rooster crowed the next morning.

It is easy to visualize Peter's mouth, gaping open after Jesus' words. It is also easy to read Peter's thoughts: That will never happen to me!

But it did happen. Peter and the other remaining apostles broke and ran when Jesus was arrested at the Garden of Gethsemane. That was bad enough! Then, the other apostles hid while Peter followed Jesus after his arrest. In the dark and chilly predawn hours, Simon Peter's faith failed repeatedly. He did, in fact, deny Jesus three times.

Fortunately, that was not the end! Though totally humiliated by his failure of faith, and quite hesitant to recommit himself (for fear of a like failure!), Peter was restored and proved to be even more effective in service for Jesus.

Lord,
Thank you that we have the freedom to fail and the grace of forgiveness and restoration. Help us to learn from our failures and to be available to our brothers and sisters who are also vulnerable.
Amen

There is great wisdom to be drawn from these events. It is naive to think that no matter how gifted, dynamic, and committed (like Peter) you might be, you cannot fail. Also, it must be recognized that such failures are often failures of faith. The good news is that, while the failure may be deeply humbling, it does not have to be final.

Most people hate to take detours, thinking they are a waste of time. Similarly, most people would see failure as a detour to success. Yet failure provides both the proper gratitude for and appreciation of success.

When Jesus Asks You to Pray

❧❧❧

Then Jesus told them a parable
about their need to pray always
and not to lose heart.

Luke 18:1

The Gospel of Hope

This poetic text reminds us of the oft-neglected virtue of hope. Every time we pray, we are practicing this virtue, for without hope we would flee from the pointless exercises of asking, seeking, knocking. Without hope, we would not pray.

Ask, and it will be given you; search, and you will find; knock, and the door will be opened for you.

Matthew 7:7

Surely this text is one of the most consoling in Scripture! How fond we are of quoting this assurance that our prayers are both heard and answered. Yet reality nips away at our confidence. Often we have asked—and not received that for which we asked. Often we have sought—and never found that for which we were looking. Often we have knocked—and not been allowed to enter. How do we explain such experiences that seem counter to the reassuring words of Jesus?

Is it possible that we may not recognize the answers to our prayers?

Perhaps God's answer is the gift of perseverance that allows us to continue to ask; perhaps the answer comes as the ingenuity to seek other solutions; perhaps the answer comes as the opening of new insights into our challenge.

Our God is a God of surprises who is dedicated to leading us toward our eternal glory, not to preserving us from pain.

Behold, I Stand at the Door *by Ludwig Haber*

Our God is an ever-creating God who is constantly nudging us to be creative and imaginative. Our God is a mischievous God who excels at camouflaging guidance as setbacks and blessings as crosses.

We need to pray, for in prayer we discover that God is not only in the answering; God is also in the asking. God is not only in the finding; God is also in the seeking. God is not only in the opening; God is also in the knocking.

I came before you in my need,
begging, pleading,
my desires to fulfill.

"Turn brass into gold
and stones into bread,"
I implored.
"Make others bend to me.
You, O Mighty One,
My wants can satisfy."

Through planet turns
and season changes
most earnestly did I entreat,
confident of my prayers' answers.

With absence of thunderbolt
or angelic announcement
the miracle was done.
Now am I satisfied.

Though no surplus of bread
nor gold have I,
nor do others bow to me,
yet transformation is realized.

The God of surprises
indulges me,
fulfilling me beyond my asking.
The miracle is within—
It is I who am changed.

The Father's Loving Generosity

Sometimes it seems our heartfelt prayers must be falling on deaf ears. Since nothing appears to be happening in response to our requests, does God the Father really want to answer our prayers?

Is there anyone among you who, if your child asks for bread, will give a stone? Or if the child asks for a fish, will give a snake? If you then, who are evil, know how to give good gifts to your children, how much more will your Father in heaven give good things to those who ask him!

Matthew 7:9–11

Father's Day is a time to remember and celebrate what fathers have contributed to their children. During the rest of the year, the focus is, from a practical standpoint, on the child and his or her needs and desires. So it seems only right that parents (including mothers) should be lovingly spotlighted from time to time.

After all, for the first 18 to 21 (or more!) years of children's lives, they are highly dependent on parents to provide for their needs. Of course, children only very gradually become aware of just how dependent they are on their parents' provision. (Some, seemingly, never do.) They are usually caught up in trying to "grow up" and declare their independence.

Because they are thoroughly preoccupied with their own personal desires or problems, they rarely give a thought to their parents' earnest hopes to meet their needs and to bond with them. Even when the parents painstakingly try to explain it, there usually is a considerable time lag before the kids really begin to understand. Rarely will a child begin to understand before the latter part of high school. Sometimes it begins to dawn on them during the college years. Most of the time, however, it is only when their own kids come along that they really begin to understand the loving generosity of their own parents.

Jesus and the Children *by Julius Schnorr von Carolsfeld*

Lord,
Thank you that you are an
infinitely caring Father,
desiring to give good gifts to
your children even more than
we want to pray for them.
Help us to pray according to
your will, which is best, and
with patience to wait on
your perfect timing.
Amen

Among the greatest tragedies in life are abusive or cold-hearted parents who do not meet their children's needs. Certainly, there are many instances in which these people are simply treating their offspring the way they were treated as kids. Sadly, that is how they learned about being a parent. As understandable as that may be, it does not diminish the tragic scars and deprivation in the lives of their own precious children.

Amazingly, there seem to be many people whose view of God the Father would be closer to a cold-hearted or even abusive parent than to the loving heavenly Father that he really is. Why is this?

There are, of course, the consistently difficult questions, such as why an all-powerful God would allow bad things to happen to seemingly good people. Beyond that, one of the most common blights on God the Father's good name has to do with prayer.

When people make sincere requests before the Father, why, so often, doesn't he answer when the request is made? As the perfect Father, God does not give his children everything they desire or ask for, since that would not help

them develop appreciation. However, he does lovingly meet all the needs of his children. As Jesus said, the heavenly Father would never be like a human parent whose child sought food and received instead a cold stone or a dangerous snake.

As the Book of James makes clear, every good gift, ultimately, comes from the heavenly Father. God does specialize in giving good gifts to those who ask him. But that must not be mistaken for some kind of heavenly credit card with no limit. God the Father is not a great big "sugar daddy" in the sky.

With wisdom we realize that just because God wants the best for us does not mean we get everything we request. The good gifts he gives us are the ones that really are good for us. That means many times he answers with something that turns out to be better than what was requested.

Wisdom also realizes that timing is everything. Our heavenly Father often does not answer prayers immediately. Instead, God is saving his perfect answer until just the right moment to introduce it into your life.

Next Father's Day, wouldn't it be appropriate to remember your heavenly Father who loves you enough to always hear you out and who gives you gifts that are perfect for you?

What's in Jesus' Name?

Have you ever researched your name in a book that gives origins and derivatives for proper names? Did the description accurately portray your character or disposition? In these two verses, we are told to pray in the name of Jesus—a name that accurately depicts his power to answer our prayers.

I will do whatever you ask in my name, so that the Father may be glorified in the Son. If in my name you ask me for anything, I will do it.

John 14:13–14

Joe is the youngest of four brothers. The older three brothers played high school football, wrestled in state championships, and excelled academically, receiving college scholarships.

When Joe entered high school, the teachers and coaches quickly recognized his last name. The football coach was delighted to have a committed player, the wrestling coach had hopes of another quality wrestler, and many teachers predicted that Joe would be as good a student as his older brothers—and they were all correct in their assumptions.

What was it about Joe's last name that caused people to take notice of him?

Jesus,
Forgive us for confiding in our own strength and looking only toward our own needs. Help us to remember to help others. When we help and welcome others, we are helping and welcoming you. Let us try to be worthy of your love. Thank you, God, for loving us. Amen

His last name carried a positive heritage, one that has sometimes been hard for him to live up to. The expectations were enormous, but Joe rose to each occasion, adding to that heritage.

What's in a name? It is a legacy, and we have the power to influence that legacy. From the beginning of time, people have recognized the link between naming and power. Among primitive peoples, as well as the ancient Hebrews, the name of a deity was regarded as his or her manifestation. Jesus or Joshua (Matthew 1:21), for example, means "Jehovah saves" in Hebrew. It is by this name that the Son of God has been worshiped by people throughout history.

When Jesus tells us to pray in his name, he is indicating that we should pray in the name of the one who has the authority to save. Now that's a power personality!

But how are we to pray?

If I win the lottery this week, I'll certainly give the church a cut. In Jesus' name. Lord, I deserve that promotion at work! In Jesus' name. Help me to make that *A* on the final exam. In Jesus' name.

I'm fairly sure this is not what Jesus had in mind. Notice the focus in each of the previous prayers. As a child, my prayers usually focused on people and things that related to me. Mother and Daddy would patiently wait as I thanked God for my family, my friends, my dog, my teachers, my toys, my lamp...in Jesus' name! I'm embarrassed that I'm not sure my prayers have changed that much.

The Resurrection *by Christian Dalsgaard*

To pray in Jesus' name is not some kind of magical invocation. Rather we are to be praying in reliance upon him. Here's a good measurement. Ask yourself this question as you pray: Will God the Father be glorified if Jesus answers this prayer in the way I desire?

If we shift our focus from us, we will experience more answered prayers. What's in Jesus' name? All the power and influence we will ever need.

Ask in My Name

Jesus provides our link for a relationship to God that comes through him but is still personal: between us and God.

Until now you have not asked for anything in my name.
Ask and you will receive, so that your joy may be complete.
John 16:24

On the night he was betrayed, Jesus spent a long evening eating and conversing with the group of friends who knew him best. After what we call the Last Supper, Jesus took the opportunity to share some final teachings with his disciples. We see a leader who knows he has to say goodbye to his followers, a friend who wants to be sure his friends are equipped to handle a world without his physical presence.

Loving God,
Thank you for sending Jesus to earth so we might know you better. Because of him, we understand your love in a new way, and we see that the door to your heart is always open. Help us, when we pray, to always pray in the spirit of Jesus Christ so that we, too, might be ready to listen to you and serve you completely. Amen

Jesus has repeatedly talked to these friends about the power of prayer, but always before he has been right beside them to pray for them and be the one through whom they understood their connection to God. Jesus knows that it is important for each person to come to a personal relationship with the Almighty. "Until now you have not asked for anything in my name. Ask and you will receive, so that your joy may be complete."

For three years, Jesus has been with most of these friends on a day-in-day-out basis. They know him, love him, trust him. They have heard his stories and know that God is like the woman searching for a lost coin, the shepherd searching for his lost sheep. Only now do they begin to understand that once Jesus is gone, God will still be with them. God's heart of love will always be open to them.

We who live long after Jesus and his friends have left the earth also need a God who personally cares for us and is available through prayer. Our joy is made complete when we connect to God in Jesus' name.

No Longer Hypocrites in Prayer

Jesus is not putting down public prayer, only showy prayer. Jesus looks at the motivation of our prayer as well as the fruits of our relationship with God.

Whenever you pray, do not be like the hypocrites; for they love to stand and pray in the synagogues and at the street corners, so that they may be seen by others.

Matthew 6:5

What is your motivation for prayer? This is the issue that Jesus is addressing. I remember hearing the late Quaker teacher and author Douglas Steere say that the purpose of prayer was to bring about change in our whole being. Prayer is not about being seen or noticed by others but about a deep relationship with God that manifests itself in deeds of kindness and words of care.

Mount Sinai

Jesus assumes you are a person of prayer and wants you to have the same intimacy with God that he shares. He has some suggestions, "Do not be like the hypocrites." Their outer actions do not correspond with the inner life of prayer. There are people who use their religion or their church attendance as a way of winning favor. They want to be seen as good and upstanding members of their community. It is good for business. It gives comfort to the family.

Jesus looks at the heart. Is there a connection between what is said and what is done? Do the words pronounced so grandly in the public arena match up with deeds of compassion and acts of justice? "What good is it, my brothers and sisters, if you say you have faith but do not have works?" (James 2:14).

Look at your prayer life. Has your relationship with God led you to be more loving? Are you trying to impress God with your prayers or are you honestly coming before God in humility and with thanksgiving? Are you finding more peace and joy in your times of prayer?

A Room for Prayer

Jesus instructs us on letting go of distraction and entering a holy space for prayer.

Whenever you pray, go into your room and shut the door and pray to your Father who is in secret.

Matthew 6:6

Worship is important, the gathering of the community of faith for encouragement and comfort. Service is important, living out our faith. Yet worship and the life of faithful actions are knit together and undergirded with personal prayer, with a personal relationship with God. Jesus says, "Shut the door and spend some time with God."

Jesus is not saying you can only pray in your room with a closed door, but he uses the image to call us to set aside a time and a place for personal prayer. Where is your quiet place to pray? What is the best time for you to pray, when you are fresh and alert? Where can you close the door on the distractions of life? I have developed a practice of going over to an empty sanctuary and spending an hour in prayer before I go sit at my desk to take care of the needs of the day. Others have a special room for meditation. Still others take a walk. Above all, Jesus is saying take time for prayer.

Besides the physical setting for prayer, Jesus is also saying we should prepare an inner room for prayer. Close the door to worry and to fear. A friend once said, "Anything worth worrying about is worth praying about." Close the door to being guarded in prayer or censoring what you think God can handle. Shut the door of the mind on mental distractions and just be with God. Still the body and quiet the mind, and spend time with the God who truly loves you.

WHAT A FRIEND WE HAVE IN JESUS

Have we trials and temptation?
Is there trouble anywhere?
We should never be discouraged;
Take it to the Lord in prayer.
Can we find a friend so faithful
who will all our sorrows share?
Jesus knows our every weakness;
take it to the Lord in prayer.

Joseph M. Scriven

Hallowed Be Thy Name

Our words of prayer may be praise, lament, petition, thanksgiving; they may be dialogue alternating with silence. But all such words we address confidently to the one, merciful, ever-listening God.

When you are praying, do not heap up empty phrases as the Gentiles do; for they think that they will be heard because of their many words.

Matthew 6:7

Those poor gentiles really had a problem! When life became burdensome and they sought heavenly assistance, they were confronted with yet one more perplexity: To which deity should they pray? For the Romans, the choices included Jupiter, Diana, Mercury, Ceres, Mars, Venus, and many others. The Egyptians could choose Amon, Isis, Re, Osiris, Seth, and more. In addition, there were the

gods and goddesses of the Assyrians, the Phoenicians, the Canaanites, the Mesopotamians, and on and on.

Choosing the correct deity was a serious matter. Perhaps Ceres isn't answering prayers today. What if Zeus isn't in a benevolent mood? Maybe Poseidon isn't listening now. How is a mere mortal to know what to do?

The only reasonable way to deal with this dilemma is to try to address all the deities. Jesus, who prayed for days in the desert, was not critical of long prayers. Rather, he was assuring his followers, and us, that we need not concern ourselves about which deity to address.

There is but one God, who is ever attentive, loving, and merciful, and whose name we are always to revere and hold sacred.

Hallowed be your name, O God! You are Creator, Yahweh, El Shaddai, Abba, Mother, Rock, Adonai, Choreographer of Galaxies.

Hallowed be your name, O God! You are Teacher, Rabbi, Good Shepherd, Savior, Wisdom Come Down.

Hallowed be your name, O God! You are Eternal Fire, Weaver of Visions, Consummate Beloved, Wellspring of Peace, Divine Stillness.

Hallowed be your name, O God! You are Love Enfleshed, Love Enflamed. You are Alpha and Omega, Yin and Yang, Immanence and Transcendence. You are Mystery. You are One.

Unity in Prayer

Praying together brings us together. When we gather in Christian community, God is with us, and suddenly we are not separate individuals but one in Jesus' name.

Again, truly I tell you, if two of you agree on earth about anything you ask, it will be done for you by my Father in heaven. For where two or three are gathered in my name, I am there among them.

Matthew 18:19–20

For me, the most powerful part of our worship service is the prayer time when we begin by sharing joys (causes for thanksgiving to God) and concerns (specific requests for God's presence and power). The congregation so firmly believes in the power of intercessory prayer that even visitors sometimes raise their hands to share what is heavy on their hearts so that the gathered community can offer prayers.

Almighty God,
Fulfill now, O Lord, our desires and petitions
as may be best for us;
granting us in this world knowledge of your truth,
and in the age to come life everlasting.

St. John Chrysostom

On any given week, there will be persons lifted up who are ill, who must face the death of a loved one, who are dealing with depression. No request is unimportant. All requests for prayers are lifted up as the community prays together.

In sharing our lives, we not only know more about each other, but we are bonded by the belief that God hears our prayers and responds. Even when the outcome is not what we want, we trust in God.

There is sometimes a palpable presence of Jesus among us. Other times, it is more like a warm feeling of being surrounded in love and understanding. But there is never any doubt that the Risen Lord stands among us.

I like the image of hot coals that when gathered together continue to provide warmth. Separate the coals and they cool. Even the most independent of us benefits from community. God didn't mean for us to go it alone!

Deliver Us From Evil Times!

The Boy Scout motto is "Be prepared." If we are praying, and as well prepared as possible, what is God's role in protecting us during very difficult times?

Be alert at all times, praying that you may have the strength to escape all these things that will take place, and to stand before the Son of Man.

Luke 21:36

Tornadoes and hurricanes are cousins. The difference is that tornadoes, comparatively, slug away in the lightweight class while hurricanes usually deliver fearsome knockout punches as super heavyweights.

For all their wind-blown power, tornado funnels swoop down from the sky, cut a narrow swath of destruction, then lift off again. However, even a short distance from where the tornado touches down may provide safety.

By contrast, hurricanes wreak havoc along and behind a front hundreds of miles long. Besides the high winds and rain, many tornadoes are spawned by hurricanes; a tornado can be the most dangerous part of the hurricane.

Fleeing from the path of a hurricane is a much bigger thing. You may have to relocate hundreds of miles to get completely out of harm's way.

The Bible realistically tells us that there are pockets of suffering that we will all have to endure. That is why Jesus wisely advises us to pray, "Deliver us from evil." Like tornadoes that come and go, there are many events that leave an evil path of destruction and pain in our lives.

Lord,
I know hard times will come. I do not ask you to deliver me from those stretching periods in my life. I only seek your strong protection from the overwhelmingly difficult times.
Amen

However, there will come a time, at the end of the age in which we are living, when suffering will be at an all-time high. For that time, or any other period of suffering, Jesus counsels alertness and prayer for escape from the most intense evil and pain.

Jesus does promise protection, though it's impossible to know exactly how that works. He will tailor the protection to each one's needs and prayers.

Jesus, Guide Us

We can ask God to lead us and guide us through each day.

✦✦✦

He came out and went, as was his custom, to the
Mount of Olives; and the disciples followed him.
When he reached the place, he said to them, "Pray
that you may not come into the time of trial."

Luke 22:39–40

✦✦✦

Most mornings I begin a time of prayer with the words of St. Francis. As I sing the words, I am asking for light, faith, hope, charity, insight, and wisdom so I might see the path of God in the day that is unfolding. It is a prayer for guidance and discernment.

Days can be packed with people to meet and decisions to be made, and throughout the day I desire the guidance of God. I want to make good decisions and treat people kindly. I want to help those in need and avoid temptations. I pray that God will guide me, lead me, protect me.

When Jesus goes out to the Mount of Olives and instructs his disciples to pray to avoid the time of trial, he is echoing his earlier instructions to pray, "Do not bring us to the time of trial" (Matthew 6:13). This can also be paraphrased, "Save us from the coming trial," or "Do not bring us to the test." They are all ways of asking God to guide us through each day. It is a way of asking God to help us discern what is the right way to go.

Another way to sharpen our discernment of God's way is to review each day, looking back over the events and giving thanks or noticing the areas where we fell short. If there is one thing that keeps coming to mind in the review, use that as a focus for prayer. Then look toward the next day and be aware of the events and feelings of anticipation. Offer what is to come to God and pray that God will guide you and keep you from trials and temptations. Close with the Lord's Prayer.

Most High and Glorious God,
Give light to the darkness of my soul.
Give me right faith, certain hope, and
*   perfect charity.*
Lord, give me insight and wisdom
So I might always discern
Your holy and true will.

When Jesus Asks You to Love

I give you a new commandment, that you love one another. Just as I have loved you, you also should love one another.

John 13:34

The Summation

Challenged to summarize the New Testament Scriptures, we would have difficulty in being more comprehensive, more inspiring, more poetic than this one sentence from the Gospel of John.

God so loved the world that he gave his only Son,
so that everyone who believes in him may not perish
but may have eternal life.

John 3:16

What would happen if every morning, noon, and night for a period of time, say a month, we thoughtfully recited this summary statement of the New Testament? What would happen if three times a day we halted in our busyness, cleared our mind of its myriad distractions, and meditated on each word or phrase of this one gospel verse?

God…so loved…the world…that he gave…his only Son…so that everyone…who believes…in him…may not perish…but may have eternal life.

God: our Loving Creator, the One Who Is and Always Will Be, Ancient Beauty, Inclusive Lover, Adonai, Holy Mystery, Uncreated Energy, Ultimate Reality, Eternal Goodness;

So loved: cherished beyond measure, boundlessly delighted in, treasured without cost, esteemed affectionately, was tenderly devoted to, lavishly prized;

The Ascension *by Anton Dorph*

The world: our earthly home, our human family, our nation, our community, my church, my family, me;

That he gave: God presented graciously, the Sacred One granted, the Source of All Good sent forth, Yahweh bestowed, the Eternal One delivered freely, the Holy One entrusted;

His only Son: Love Enfleshed, Lamb of God, Light of the World, God Incarnate, Savior, Wisdom Come Down, Key of David, Crucified Divinity;

So that everyone: all people, each and every one of us, my enemies, my family and friends, I myself;

Who believes: who recognizes, accepts, rejoices in, follows, becomes a disciple of, puts faith in, relies on, places confidence in, trusts;

In him: in Jesus the Christ, in the Good News of Jesus, in the Incarnation and the Resurrection, in the Word, in the Easter Miracle, in the Way and the Truth and the Life;

May not perish: will not be separated from God, will have their names written in the Book of Life, will not be lost, will not be deprived of the all-consuming union with God;

But may have eternal life: will be united forever with God, will spend eternity in the beatific vision, will enjoy eternal glory, will be in the presence of God's perfect love forever.

God is love, and those who abide in love abide in God, and God abides in them.

1 John 4:16

However, a word of warning: Meditating upon this text daily should be undertaken only if you are willing to risk change most profound! To immerse ourselves in contemplating the extent of God's love is a hazardous endeavor, for such a task is opening ourselves to an encounter with the Holy. We become vulnerable to moments of grace, when, being filled with the Spirit, we just may fall in love with the Divine Beloved.

Such a love affair challenges us not only to return that love to God but also to spread that love to the world. Encountering Love Unbounded is dangerous, for we may be jolted out of our complacency, never to return. Dare we risk it?

Put Your Heart Into It

Jesus came not to destroy the old commandments but to fulfill and amplify them. He boiled down all the regulations of the law of Moses into a new commandment found in these verses: We are to love God with everything we are and have.

And one of them, a lawyer, asked him a question to test him. "Teacher, which commandment in the law is the greatest?" He said to him, "'You shall love the Lord your God with all your heart, and with all your soul, and with all your mind.' This is the greatest and first commandment."

Matthew 22:35–38

Have you ever seen this bumper sticker? *God said it. I believe it. That settles it.* I'm always a little put off by this message. Is it suggesting that God doesn't expect us to use our minds? Should we avoid questions in favor of blind faith?

I believe Matthew 22:35-38 speaks to this argument. Here Jesus indicates that we are to use everything we are—our hearts, souls, and minds—to love God. Perhaps a better phrase would be: *God loves me. I believe it. That settles it.*

While there is much debate over the interpretation of these three parts of a person, let's assume that heart represents the emotional, inner feeling part of ourselves; that soul represents the spiritual, God-conscious component; and that mind represents our intellectual thought capacity.

When I read these verses, I find it much easier to love God in the reverse order of Jesus' statement. In a western culture that primarily identifies itself with linguistic and logical modes of thinking,

it is not surprising that loving God with my mind seems to be the easiest of the three. Obviously we can use our minds to study God's Word, the writings of church historians, and inspirational material (like this book!). We can all think thoughts of love and appreciation for God without much effort.

As I meditated on these verses, for example, and focused on how much I love God, I thought about all he has done for me, the ways he has guided my life, and his words of love in the Scriptures to me. I concluded that I love God because he first loved me, and that his is a great big love that has provided a way for imperfect me to live eternally with the Perfect One.

To love God with my soul or spiritual side has not seemed so difficult either. Maybe that's because I have a God who is pursuing a love relationship with me! Growing up in a home where my parents loved God helped create in me the spiritual values of church attendance, Bible study, development and

use of my spiritual gifts, and more. Early in my childhood, I felt God's stirring in my soul, drawing me toward him through his love. After 40 years of spiritual development, I've learned I can best love God with all my soul by obeying his Word and worshiping him with a community of believers.

This brings me to Jesus' first charge—to love God with all my heart. Certainly Jesus expects me to be rational and vigorous in my love for God. Unfortunately, I often unconsciously interpret his command to mean that I am to love God as a mere act of the will without any emotional attachment. After all, the Greek verb for love in these verses is not *phileo,* which means friendly affection, but *agapao,* the commitment of devotion.

Yet, in normal ancient Greek usage, *agape* had a number of meanings, including "to long for" or "to prefer." Do I long for God as a child longs for a parent? I have to admit that sometimes my heart just isn't in it. And I suspect that I am not the only person who often wonders, "Why don't I feel love toward God?"

What many of us are experiencing is a fragmented love. Somehow, we have to find a way to integrate the longing of our spirits and minds with our innermost, heartfelt feelings.

My husband, Stan, and I were very good friends for a long time before we fell in love. We attended the same university, played tennis together, and spent a lot of time together in a college Bible study group. After a year of intimate friendship, the idea of what it might be like to be in love with Stan began creeping into my thoughts on a regular basis. Those invasive thoughts led to a longing to be with

O Love, were I but love,
And could I but love you, Love, with love!
O Love, for love's sake, grant that I,
Having become love, may know Love wholly as Love!
   Hadewijch of Belgium, a 13th-Century mystic

Stan. Once that desire was reciprocated, we began to experience more heart-intensive feelings for each other. In fact, we couldn't get enough time together, and our relationship was (and continues to be) characterized by challenging

each other's mind, spirit, and passion.

In the same way, spending time with God enriches and deepens our relationship with him. The more we get to know him and experience his love, the more we will be able to love him with our entire being. Then we will long for time alone with him, because we love him and enjoy his fellowship.

Maybe one of the reasons Jesus commanded us to first love God with all our hearts is because he knows that a deep, inner relationship must set the tone for loving God with our souls and minds. It is not enough to think about loving God. It is not enough to believe that we should love God. It is not enough to work at proving our love for God. But if we open ourselves up to a love relationship with God, I believe our hearts will be transformed and we will begin to experience the passion for him that Jesus commanded.

Loving Obedience

Our love for Jesus manifests itself in our thoughts, words, and actions. When we truly love him, how we should act becomes clear. Even when we feel tempted to do the less-than-loving thing, we can remember Jesus' love for us and follow his example.

If you love me, you will keep my commandments.

John 14:15

Four-year-old Flora is the kind of kid who makes people glad just to be alive when they see her shining face. Strangers must look at her and think, "Today's a good day, after all." Flora is good at hugs and verbal affirmations. She takes time with people, looks deep into their eyes, and listens carefully to their responses.

Flora frequently bounces into my office, full of energy and questions about God. One day she said, "I asked my dad what a minister does and he said you teach about God." I nodded. "That's a big part of my job."

Flora looked serious. "I want to teach about God when I grow up." I hugged her to me. "Oh, Flora, you already do teach about God." "I do?" she asked. "You are so full of love and goodness, how can people not know God if they know you?" I answered.

She chortled with delight, then bounced out of my office back to the nursery school playground. I sat, realizing the truth of what I had said to her: What a difference we can make to the world when our love shines out from us! I can't help

If there is any kindness I can show, or any good thing I can do to any fellow being, let me do it now, and not deter or neglect it, as I shall not pass this way again.

William Penn

but think that Jesus was the sort of person whose presence made ordinary people feel special, unreligious types want to know God, the unrighteous yearn for justice. His very life was an example of what it means to follow all the commandments.

And so, when he tells us, "If you love me, you will keep my commandments," we know that only by such obedience do we really show our love. Sure, there are difficult people we find hard to love. That's when we let Jesus love through us until our own love develops. There will be situations where it would be easiest to fudge a bit on our calling ("I won't point out that the salesclerk gave me too much change," "I'll pretend I didn't hear that racist joke," "If I cheat on my wife just this once . . ."). But our love for Jesus holds us to keep his commandments.

When you love you should not say, "God is in my heart," but rather, "I am in the heart of God."

Kahlil Gibran

Is there someone you find difficult to love? Imagine Jesus in that person. Make an effort to discover something lovable about them that might not be easily visible. Pray for the person so that you might feel connected to them through the spirit of Jesus, who came that they—as well as you—might know God.

Are there other commandments that you find hard to honor? Find strength in Jesus who loved you so much he was willing to die for you. If God was able to raise Jesus from the dead, then certainly God can provide you with the wherewithal to stand strong in your beliefs.

Believe in Jesus. Live like Jesus. Love is enough.

Love God, Love Others

If we love God, we are led to love others. The two go hand in hand and lead us to some surprising ministries.

✦✦✦

When they had finished breakfast, Jesus said to Simon Peter, "Simon son of John, do you love me more than these?" He said to him, "Yes, Lord; you know that I love you." Jesus said to him, "Feed my lambs."

John 21:15

✦✦✦

I learned a lot about loving service from my parents. Their Christian faith was not a "Sundays Only" practice. They lived it all through the week, and as a young kid I sometimes found that difficult. Often my Mom would bake three apple pies. The smell would fill the whole house, and I would dream of eating my favorite pie for days, only to discover that Mom was taking one to a neighbor and another to a church potluck. I would be left to share one with my parents and my brother and sister.

Many of the Christmas cookies disappeared the same way. There was always some for me, though maybe not as many as my greedy eyes desired. I look back now and give thanks that my parents modeled sharing. I sometimes joke with Mom that she took literally the words of Jesus, "Feed my lambs."

Jesus and Scripture are clear that love of God should lead to loving action. If we love God, then we will love others. Indeed, when Jesus was summing up the commandments, he clearly linked these two: "You shall love the Lord your God with all your heart, and with all your soul, and with all your mind. . . . You shall love your neighbor as yourself" (Matthew 22:37–39).

Compassionate God,
Give us eyes to see those who are in need,
and make our hearts tender to the pain around us.

Give us a patient persistence to see that justice is done
and fill us with a gentle courage to care when it would be easier to turn away.

Teach us, Loving God, to follow the compassionate steps of your Son,
who so loved us that we might share love with others.
Amen

Loving service will sometimes take us to people and places we don't expect. Peter did not expect to take Christianity to gentiles, but being nudged in a dream and receiving the visitors sent by Cornelius (Acts 10) led him to a dramatic change. "I truly understand that God shows no partiality, but in every nation anyone who fears him and does what is right is acceptable to him" (Acts 10:34–35). God's love crosses all boundaries and such a vision has sent doctors, teachers, plumbers, and builders all over the world to extend love and care to people in need.

Loving service takes us to forgotten people. Friends of mine have started a summer week of camp for people with AIDS. Ministers, nurses, and volunteers create a week of fun, relaxation, and worship for people who may not be around to enjoy the next summer. A church youth group visits a nursing home and discovers that one of the kids, who is often in trouble, has a real knack for befriending the residents in their wheelchairs.

It all starts with the love of God and learning to listen to whom God would have you love. "Do you love me? Feed the hungry, care for the sick, embrace the forgotten, care for the homeless, love the unlovable."

Loving Your Enemies Is Healthy

It is at least as common to hear a small child scream "I hate you!" as to hear "I love you!" Why should you even try to change something that is so deep-seated in the human personality?

❧❧❧

You have heard that it was said, "You shall love your neighbor and hate your enemy." But I say to you, Love your enemies and pray for those who persecute you.

Matthew 5:43–44

❧❧❧

I n Jesus' day, the people heard from the great teachers of their society that they were to love their neighbors, meaning their families and their friends and others living nearby. In teaching this principle, the rabbis were doing no more than applying the straightforward wording of the Hebrew Bible.

So far, so good. But some teachers did not stop there. It was undoubtedly their observation of human nature that convinced them that hating enemies was acceptable. But the Bible never has given the okay on such hatred.

This appears to be one of those cases where the conventional wisdom wins out over time. Perhaps there was a good bit of initial hesitancy to make the jump from loving those on your side to hating those on the opposing side, as logical as it sounded. But eventually the natural tendency of human nature won out. It came to the point where hating those who hate you made as much sense to the bulk of society as loving those who love you.

From a nearsighted perspective, that may pass for wisdom. Jesus, however, knew better. Hatred is unwise both because it is wrong and it is unhealthy. Certainly, the Bible observes a large number of cases in which people hate one another. Though there are many occasions in which

Lord,
I don't like the idea of not
being able to hate my enemy.
Still, I need your forgiveness
and I ask that you help me
love that person, as I pray on
their behalf.
Amen

no comment is made as to the rightness or wrongness of the hatred, that does not mean the Scriptures are quiet.

There are no situations in which interpersonal hatred is considered right (even if it is understandable). There are, however, enough instances in which the hate is clearly labeled as wrong to get the point. Whenever the Bible chooses to speak to the issue, it leaves no doubt that one person hating another is wrong.

Yet, there is one broad category in which hatred is always right. But it still does not allow for hating other people. Rather, proper hatred is hating sin. That means hating the act, but not the actor; hating that which is done in violation of God's gracious standards, not hating the person who commits the sinful action.

That, of course, is not an easy thing to do. It almost seems like splitting hairs to try to tell the difference between what has been done and who does it. After all, the wrongful action would not have happened if the person involved had not chosen to act.

It appears that God has wisely laid out this distinction between sin and sinner for two important reasons. First, the Lord hates the sin, but does not hate the sinner. Thus, for human beings to do likewise is to choose to be in God's camp and to reflect in their lives a truly divine perspective.

Second, and very significant psychologically, hating the act but not the actor provides a way to channel the outrage that is felt. That, of course, is no small thing. It is possible to defuse hate, but it is much more common to internalize it. How much better to properly express the outrage as hatred of an

action than to bury it inside as a virtual volcano of bitterness toward the person performing the act.

Jesus corrected the improper assertion with his own authoritative command. Loving your enemies, including those who persecute you, is a tall order. It is much easier to give in to hate. However, it is clearly the right thing to do; both psychologically and physically, it is the healthy thing to do.

It is no longer a mystery why bitter people are more likely to experience heart disease, ulcers, and other physical complications. There is a tremendous amount of internal stress related to hatred. It is not too much to say that hatred-induced stress eats a person up from the inside out.

Physical problems, premature aging, and as a worst-case scenario, death before your time is an incredibly steep price to pay for hatred. That remains true no matter what some enemy has done to you.

It should be realized, though, that Jesus is not just asking for a releasing or refocusing of the hatred that is felt toward enemies. He is also insisting on loving prayer for the person you would much rather despise. If choosing not to hate is a tall order, this assignment is at least as high as the top of a skyscraper!

There is an angle, or at least a perspective, that can make that kind of prayer somewhat easier. Releasing hatred of your enemy, or even someone you care about, requires forgiveness. That is very difficult, but it should be remembered that the person seething with hatred requires forgiveness also.

Think about it. Hatred is sinful, and, in committing that sin, you have become an enemy of God's standards. And if you must ask God's forgiveness for the sin of bitter hatred, how can you, in good conscience, withhold forgiveness from your enemy.

Hating your enemy requires you to pray to the Lord, asking his forgiveness. So, while you're at it, you might as well go ahead and pray for the enemy who has stirred up your hate. The words may choke in your heart, if not your throat, as you attempt to express your prayer. The prayer may not be heartfelt initially, but go ahead and do it anyway.

Always remember that it is the right thing, the loving thing, the wise thing to do, almost miraculously so. Also, understand that the Lord will respond to your prayers by eventually enabling you to really love that previously unlovable enemy.

We love because he first loved us. Those who say, "I love God," and hate their brothers or sisters, are liars; for those who do not love a brother or sister whom they have seen, cannot love God whom they have not seen. The commandment we have from him is this: those who love God must love their brothers and sisters also.

1 John 4:19–21

Proper Self-Love Overflows

Self-love has gotten the bad name of being the same thing as selfishness. If you cannot love yourself, however, it is practically impossible to love others. But how can you tell the difference between self-love and selfishness?

He said to him, "'You shall love the Lord your God with all your heart, and with all your soul, and with all your mind.' This is the greatest and first commandment. And a second is like it: 'You shall love your neighbor as yourself.' On these two commandments hang all the law and the prophets."

Matthew 22:37–40

Narcissism is a big word for total self-centeredness, egomania, and self-absorption. A few years ago it was referred to as "being stuck on yourself."

It is ironic that in recent times our culture seems to be filled with both highly insecure people and those who are convinced they are a gift to humanity. Although these seem like opposite personality defects, they both stem from an imbalance in how you love yourself.

Jesus had been asked what the greatest commandment was in the Jewish biblical law. He carefully considered all the commands of the Hebrew Bible, which number over 700. After surveying the various possibilities, he wisely determined that the greatest of all the commands is to love God and a close second is to love your neighbor as you love yourself.

The two work together, hand in hand. The second command is designed to play off the first commandment. The first commandment is the vertical dimension, between God and humankind. It is designed to provide a spiritual anchor for your life. The second is its horizontal counterpart, person to person. It is designed to promote the best and most supportive kind of human relationships.

Lord,
Help me to love you and to
love myself in a healthy
way, not selfishly, so that I
may be able to love those
close to me in a way that
will encourage and enrich
them.
Amen

No one other than Jesus has ever been able to keep all 700 commandments, since nobody's perfect except Jesus. Yet, it is possible even for us fallible humans to obey the heart of the first commandment. Not only are loving God and loving your neighbor as yourself the Lord's greatest commands, together they also summarize the rest of the 700 commandments. Each of the other commands can, in some sense, be categorized as having to do with either loving God or loving others as you love yourself. So there is a lot riding on these two spotlighted commands, which could be called the Two-Step Program (more streamlined than Twelve Steps).

Still, as simple and straightforward as Jesus' two great commandments are, they are far from easy to carry out. That is especially true if a person is attempting to generate proper love for God, self-love, and love for others with his or her own abilities.

Fortunately, that does not have to happen. You see, God is the one who first initiated love toward humankind, and he continues to do so. He loved us first, and he always loves us perfectly. So our first responsibility (commandment) is to love him back, much like a child learns to do toward a loving parent.

As individuals come to understand that the Creator God of the universe is their loving heavenly Father, they realize that they are lovable, *love-ly,* to the One whose opinion counts most of all. Realizing that you are considered worthy of receiving love makes it a lot easier to love yourself, which protects against a deflated view of self.

Still, this sense of being perfectly loved and having great significance in God's eyes must be seen in context, lest it be taken to an egotistical extreme. It must always be remembered that you are not an only child. Much like an only child who has been lavished with so much, if God's children have on blinders, they can easily have an overly inflated view of self.

Christ and the Children *by Bernard Plockhorst*

God has many children who have received his wondrous love through Jesus Christ. He loves each one perfectly and never plays favorites. Yet, he also loves each one realistically, meaning he recognizes their weaknesses and limitations along with their unique strengths and talents.

Knowing that God loves in such a perfectly balanced way makes it easier for us to accept ourselves, warts and all. If he who understands us better than we understand ourselves can still love us unconditionally, we certainly can learn to love ourselves. The all-knowing and all-wise God would never waste his love on someone who wasn't worth it. Some of us are better able to internalize his love and to love in return or in reflection of God's love.

Obviously, someone who is

starving from a lack of nutrition will not possess much energy with which to work or do other activities. If anything, that person's attention will be consumed with the basic need of trying to find food to satisfy hunger. Likewise, a person who is starving for love is grasping to meet his or her personal needs and has very little in reserve with which to love others.

Narcissistic people are so caught up in loving themselves that they see no need to love others. On the other hand, people who have not experienced love are preoccupied with simply trying to fill the hole in their hearts and are almost unable to get beyond that.

So, while Jesus' wisdom is expressed as commands, not suggestions, he realizes that loving others is harder for some people than others. In the end, though, love is not just a fleeting feeling. If that were the case, love would never last any longer than the next time you were exhausted or there was emotional upheaval. It would always be "here today, gone tomorrow."

Instead, true love is at least as much a choice as an emotion. It is, at the root, choosing to seek the best for the one being loved, however challenging that might be at times. Thus, loving your neighbor is a choice, a wise choice, that God expects you to make, no matter how you feel about yourself. But he also offers his perfect love as a balancing factor to help you wisely avoid the extremes of being overly self-critical or pompously self-centered.

A Friend in Need

How can the love of a friend endure the worst of times as well as flourish in the best of times?

Jesus began to weep. So the Jews said, "See how he loved him!"
John 11:35–36

Many of us have heard the saying, "A friend in need is a friend indeed." Friends you have only been through good times with are untested friends. However, it would be premature to label such people "fair-weather friends" simply because you haven't faced the foul weather of life yet. Likewise, should you write off someone as a "fair-weather friend" if they aren't there at the beginning of your troubles? There are many reasons why a friend might not come immediately.

But what are we to make of Jesus' delay in coming to help Lazarus? He was a distance away when he heard about his friend's illness. Still, he did not go immediately upon receiving the news.

Jesus raises Lazarus.

In fact, Jesus arrived after Lazarus' funeral. His friend's body had already been in the tomb for several days. While Jesus' tears before the tomb indicated the depth of his loving friendship for Lazarus, some onlookers understandably questioned Jesus' tardy arrival.

It is difficult to understand why Jesus did not appear in time to help before Lazarus died. Yet Lazarus' dead body offered the opportunity for Jesus to perform a miracle of resurrection, previewing his own coming back from the dead. Beyond the grief of their loss, Lazarus' sisters and friends experienced the joy of getting him back.

And so it is with our lives. The first wave of friends often disappears just as the numbness and shock begin to give way to so many confusing emotions. It is the friend, like Jesus, who is there for you in this even more difficult "foul-weather" phase that qualifies with flying colors as a friend indeed.

There may be considerations why a loving friend might not appear early. But when the dust settles from life's stormiest hours, the loving friend will be there when needed most.

Lord,
Enable me to be the kind of friend who weeps when my friends weep and who rejoices when they rejoice.
Amen

When Jesus Asks You Not to Worry

❧

So do not worry about tomorrow, for tomorrow will bring worries of its own. Today's trouble is enough for today.

Matthew 6:34

God Will Provide

Jesus promises that God will provide for all our needs. When we spend time worrying, we doubt God's power to work in our lives. It's up to us to give our best effort and then trust in God to care for us.

Do not worry about your life, what you will eat or what you will drink, or about your body, what you will wear. Is not life more than food, and the body more than clothing?

Matthew 6:25

Jesus understands our mundane worries about food, shelter, and clothing. While the people he walked with didn't have to think about health insurance premiums, income taxes, and pension plans, those who lived at that "simpler" time needed reminding that life is more than food, and the body is more than clothing.

A year's sabbatical spent in a Quaker community provided just such a reminder for our family. My husband and I, along with our daughter, took a year to be students of the spiritual life instead of pastors. We went from two full-time incomes to no income. We left a three-bedroom home in California for two rooms in a large house at the Pennsylvania Quaker center. We put most of our earthly belongings in a one-hundred square foot self-storage space, packing our Honda Civic only with what we needed to live for a year with our three-year-old daughter and our soon-to-be-born son.

Talk about simplifying! For music, we packed our ten favorite tapes, and we chose a small sampling of books to get us through the year. Most of the items we thought necessary for our daughter's infancy had long since been sold, but when our son was born we managed just fine without them.

Happiness resides not in possessions and not in gold; the feeling of happiness dwells in the soul.

Democritus

One of our "new" rooms was furnished with three beds and a dresser. The other was a "great room": kitchen (hotplate and crockpot), dining room (table and chairs), living room (couch), study (desk), and guest room (mattress on the floor).

Do we remember that as a year of hardship? Absolutely not! We remember the way the sun streamed through large windows in both rooms, the generosity of the Quaker community, the joy of a newborn child, and the wonder of a preschooler. During the year, we had very few moments of wanting more things. In some ways, it was a burden to come back to the storage space and a three-bedroom home.

Money is not required to buy one necessity of the soul.
Henry David Thoreau

That sabbatical year was a perfect chance for us to immerse ourselves in the goodness of God's generosity. The goal of that year was to focus on God's presence in our lives. We were the lilies in the field, the sparrows in the air, the creatures God cared for. We learned to trust that God would provide for us. Rather than spending time worrying about money, we did our part (finding part-time work, letting churches know we were available to speak) and then we "let go and let God" provide.

If you feel anxious, take time to sit in a restful place and watch the birds. Do they look worried? Learn from their joyous living. Admire the flowers. Isn't the span of their days beautiful? So why not trust that our generous God will know our needs and care for us all our days?

Worried to Death

In a world plagued with fear of growing old, Jesus' words regarding worry are timeless. He encourages us to seek the spiritual benefits of belonging to God, including contentment in the knowledge that he knows the length of our days.

And can any of you by worrying add a single hour to your span of life?

Matthew 6:27

As the TV blared in the background, I picked up the phone. I think my heart was pounding louder than the bellowing of the TV. As I expected, my doctor was at the other end of the line. "Your biopsy report came back, and I have some bad news." I'm sure anyone who has heard those words can empathize with my response—shock, fear, tears, loss, grief, concern, worry—though not necessarily in that order.

I have spent most of my life worrying. I worried about my health, my family, what other people think, what to wear tomorrow, what I will have for dinner, the future, old age, even my little dog, Thera. When I turned 35, my deepest thoughts were, "My life is half over, and I still have so much I want to do!"

A year later, I was diagnosed with cancer and I angrily (and mistakenly) imagined God saying, "I'll give you something to worry about!" Most of my previous worries and fears were unfounded. Now I faced the real possibility of a terminal illness and I took a long, hard look inward.

GOD HOLDS THE FUTURE

God holds the future,
He's got a plan,
there's no need to worry,
'cause it's all in His hand.
So if you are strugglin'
with what you should do,
God holds the future for you.
David Meece and Brown Bannister

For the next several weeks as I prepared for surgery, I began to realize that the length of my life was well beyond my control, and surprisingly, peace settled over me like a cozy warm quilt. It was a disarming calmness; I could trust God and allow him to hold my life in his hand. Worrying was futile. It could not change my illness nor my situation. I could not add one hour to my life by worrying.

All my previous worrying did not prevent a diagnosis of cancer. In fact, the medical professionals tell us we may even be subtracting time from our lives through worry and stress. The physical results of anxiety are thought to be elevated blood pressure, increased risk of heart disease, digestive problems, and more. I decided that after the surgery, I would make a good recovery and put worrying about the life-threatening disease out of my mind.

As I lay in the hospital bed, drowsy from a morphine drip, the phone rang. Again it was my doctor's voice. "I have the reports back from your surgery. The cancer was contained and no additional treatment is necessary."

Relief did not really settle in until weeks later as I began to realize I was going to live—at least for a little while longer. The weeks of recovery

AMAZING GRACE
(4th & 5th stanzas)

Thru many dangers, toils and snares,
I have already come!
'Tis grace hath brought me safe thus far,
And grace will lead me home.

When we've been there ten thousand years,
Bright shining as the sun,
We've no less days to sing God's praise
Than when we'd first begun.

John Newton; John P. Rees, stanza 5

following surgery gave me plenty of time to reflect on how to live in the present rather than worrying about dying in the future.

I think living without worry comes with practice. Perhaps we should examine what it is that prevents us from trusting God to help us cope with our life and death. Then, when we find ourselves worrying, let it serve as a reminder that we are trusting ourselves and our own abilities rather than trusting God.

Are you worried and in distress today? Whether you're troubled about something big or small, worrying won't change your situation. Jesus does not say that bad things will not happen to us, but he does invite us to rest in his arms. As we trust God to carry the burdens of our health, families, finances, and so on, we can discover the comfort, security, and peace of knowing that God takes care of his own.

"I rebel against death, yet I know that it is how I respond to death's inevitability that is going to make me less or more fully alive."

Madeleine L'Engle, The Summer of the Great-Grandmother

What Have We Got to Lose?

Choosing to live the gospel message is challenging. Responding to the call to follow Jesus has always been—and will always be—demanding. But why are we so afraid of the sacrifices that might be asked of us?

Are not two sparrows sold for a penny? Yet not one of them will fall to the ground apart from your Father. And even the hairs of your head are all counted. So do not be afraid; you are of more value than many sparrows.

Matthew 10:29–31

We are important to God—he knows all that we think and all that we do. He cares for us well beyond what we can understand. Christ tells us this and reassures us of our value and God's protection. No matter what happens, we can rest, for our welfare is in God's loving hands. If even the lowly sparrow has a place in God's heart, then we, who have been created in God's own image, need not doubt our divine safeguard!

Jesus has invited us to come and follow. Yet, our response to Christ's call is hesitant, cautious. Holding back from enthusiastically entering his way of life, we stammer out one excuse after another. And we worry.

We worry about what others will say of us if we try to live the gospel message. "Do not be afraid," Christ responds. We worry about our financial security and future needs and safety. "Do not be afraid," Christ assures us.

We worry about our family, about its stability and unity, about family peace and love. "Do not be afraid," Christ counters. We worry about our educational plans and training programs, our jobs and careers, about our fringe benefits and retirement plans. "Do not be afraid," Christ answers.

We worry about our material possessions, our homes and cars and fancy recreational playthings. "Do not be afraid," Christ responds. We worry about our health and the well-being of those close to us. "Do not be afraid," Christ assures us.

We worry about the economy and inflation, the stock market and social security, marketing trends and getting the latest fashion craze. "Do not be afraid," Christ replies. We worry about nuclear armament and global warming and environmental pollution, the breakup of colonial realms, the merging of new alliances. "Do not be afraid," Christ responds.

Worry is the toll extracted by our poverty of faith.

We worry about failure, about whether we can possibly live up to such an ideal as that set before us in the gospel. "Do not be afraid," Christ tells us. We worry about death, about what will come before, about what will come after. "Do not be afraid," Christ answers.

We even worry about our worrying and its effect on us! "Do not be afraid," Christ says.

Repeatedly, Jesus calls us to follow him, reminding us that though our way may have problems, our ultimate good is assured. God created us out of love and will continue to care for us out of that same love. So we are not to worry nor be afraid. When all things become known, we will be surprised to discover how much attention God, who looks after the insignificant sparrows of the air and the lilies of the field, has given us throughout our lives.

So, we have nothing to lose in following Christ.

Cold Feet

A talent in Jesus' day was worth about two years' wages. Today, we don't think of a talent as money, but it is just as valuable. Each of us is given talents and opportunities, but fear can prevent us from investing our gifts.

The one who had received the one talent also came forward, saying, "Master, I knew that you were a harsh man, reaping where you did not sow, and gathering where you did not scatter seed; so I was afraid, and I went and hid your talent in the ground."

Matthew 25:24–25

The Poudre River was running high due to melting snow in the higher elevations of the Colorado Rockies. The air was brisk as we fastened our life jackets and listened to the guide's instructions. As I stepped into the raft, ice-cold water was already seeping in and numbing my feet. We pushed off with our seasoned guide steering behind us.

At first, the Class III river was fairly smooth, just a few gentle rapids. But as we approached a bend, I could hear the excited screams of the groups in front of us. We rounded the bend, and the river seemed to pick up our raft and throw it through a narrow pass. We paddled hard, but the raft slammed us against the rocks causing a huge wave to crash over my side. I felt myself sliding out of the raft. I dropped my paddle to grab onto something or someone to stay in the raft. By some miracle, the next wave pitched me hard, back to the floor of the raft. In seconds, I was completely drenched, and my legs were up to my shins in icy water.

I scrambled back to my spot and continued paddling. The water left me shaking with cold and no feeling in my feet or legs. I was so terrified that I have forgotten much about the rest of the run. When we reached the take-out point, I climbed out of the raft, ripped off the life jacket, and headed for the bus. As we drove back up Poudre Canyon for the second run, my friends asked why I had taken off my life jacket. "There's no way I'm doing that again," I replied. "I can't do it. I'm too scared. I've got cold feet in more ways than one!"

"You do look sort of pale," they noted. Inside I was paralyzed. Fear had a tight grip. I didn't know if I was shaking from the cold or from trauma.

The bus pulled up to the point where we had put the rafts in for the first run. I stepped off the bus and watched our group laughing and scrambling down the bank to the rafts at the edge of the river. Can I muster enough courage to make a second run? There's nothing wrong with admitting my fear and staying here, but what will I miss if I stay behind?

To fear is one thing. To let fear grab you by the tail and swing you around is another.

Katherine Paterson,
Jacob Have I Loved

Quickly I snapped on my life jacket, scrambled down the bank, and climbed into the raft, hardly believing I was going to take the risk. I braced myself for the first white water and paddled like a maniac. We screamed as the water hit us head on, we outmaneuvered the other rafts in water fights, and we picked up a floating log for a ceremony at the end of the run. This time, as I stepped onto dry land, I did so with a spirit of confidence and joy in mastering the river—and my fear!

In Matthew 25, Jesus told a parable about a man who was paralyzed by fear. We can't get around it—serving Jesus requires some risks. We can allow fear to clutch us, or we can admit our fears, summon our courage, make the most of our talents, and rejoice in the furthering of his kingdom.

Faith to Face Natural Fears

Some people feel fear at the drop of a hat. Yet, as extreme as that sounds, it is even more unnatural not to feel fear at all. From the standpoint of wisdom, what is the proper role of fear?

But the angel said to the women, "Do not be afraid; I know that you are looking for Jesus who was crucified. He is not here; for he has been raised, as he said."

Matthew 28:5–6

What is fear, anyway? The dictionary describes it as a distressing emotion or anxiety in the face of impending (or at least possible) pain or danger. This definition seems a little narrow, however. After all, even an unexpected "Boo!" is enough to hit the fear nerve with many people.

In not a few cases, almost anything unexpected will spark fear. In such situations, it seems that the fear is a hair-trigger dreading of the worst-case

Three Angels *by Bartolommeo di Giovanni*

scenario. People who exhibit ongoing fear, even if for limited periods of time, have fearful personalities.

At the time the women headed to the tomb of Jesus early that Sunday morning, the apostles were fearfully huddled behind closed doors. They were in hiding because they were afraid of being arrested by the Jewish authorities who had sentenced Jesus to death just days before.

Clearly, these women were not paralyzed by chronic fearfulness. They possessed the courage and faith to go and pay their respects at the earliest possible moment. Going there on the Jewish Sabbath would have been improper for them, from Friday at sundown to Saturday at sundown, or overnight, from Saturday evening to Sunday at dawn. Nevertheless, nothing was going to stop them as soon as it was permissible.

These women lived in a society that exhibited a curiosity about whether angels exist (as do many people today) and with a strong belief that angels were very active in the affairs of humankind. Most of Jewish society in that day (except the religious group called the Sadducees) firmly believed in the resurrection of the dead.

Lord,
Whether I admit it or not, I
am fearful. Please help me
to face my fears head-on
and then to act in faith.
Amen

Also, in thinking of the resurrection, there had been the teaching of Jesus. Not only did he teach the truthfulness of the resurrection in general, he had also raised several people from the dead during his ministry. There had been the son of the widow in Nain, then Jairus' daughter, and finally Jesus' close friend Lazarus. Further, Jesus stated repeatedly that he himself would be killed and raised from the dead.

Thus, it was definitely not the idea of angels, the raising of the dead, or even the resurrection of Jesus that shook up the women. Rather, the reality of the angel and the empty tomb caught them off guard. When they encountered the actuality of what they believed, it took their breath away.

Some people would say that you don't really have faith or confidence if you feel fear at any point. That sort of fearlessness is, unfortunately, an unrealistic expectation for most people. For example, even the most polished and confident athletes and speakers frequently admit to still feeling "butterflies" in their stomachs just hours prior to going on stage. Sometimes, such stars will even go so far as to say that they would think something was very wrong if they weren't feeling the fear to some extent. So, if such accomplished masters of their fields are typically nervous and fearful, why should the rest of us be embarrassed or sheepish when we feel the same thing?

Morning of the Resurrection *by Sir Edward Burne-Jones*

Let's face it. The real argument is not whether someone should be fearful. Fear, to some extent, is a completely natural response. Rather, the question should be about what a person does when they feel fear, when their pulse and breathing quicken, when the hair stands up on the back of the neck.

The wisdom that comes from Jesus is to use the natural fear as a springboard to faith. Not only does the Bible recognize the common reality of fear in our lives, the Hebrew Scriptures frequently even refer to what is often called faith as fear: "the fear of the Lord." This terminology certainly has to do partly with respecting the greatness and holiness of God. A healthy fear of the rightful Judge of the universe is a positive thing.

However, it is highly unlikely that respect, no matter how great, is the full meaning of the fear of the Lord. Instead, this key concept almost surely includes focusing the natural fear you are feeling toward the Lord. You can do so, not only realizing that he deserves your respectful fear, but also trusting that he will calm your fears regarding any dangers in your life.

It is unlikely that many of us will ever stand face to face with an angel or walk into a graveyard and be informed that a resurrection has taken place. Yet, there will inevitably be surprises, shocks, or dangers that will stir up fear in each of our lives. In wisdom, we must put aside the question of why we are fearful. We must concentrate on channeling the fear in the direction of the Lord, who will put our emotions in the calm eye of the storm.

Faith Overcomes Fear

Jesus understands our fears and wants us to know that no matter what happens in our lives, he is with us. When we believe in his power, fear has no hold on us.

Jesus himself stood among them and said to them, "Peace be with you." They were startled and terrified, and thought that they were seeing a ghost. He said to them, "Why are you frightened, and why do doubts arise in your hearts? Look at my hands and my feet; see that it is I myself. Touch me and see; for a ghost does not have flesh and bones as you see that I have."

Luke 24:36–39

During a Bible study, one of my parishioners commented about the disciples. "They actually lived with Jesus, knew him personally, heard him firsthand. Yet still, they constantly misunderstood him. Their faith was so small. You'd think you'd stay on your toes if you were hanging out with Jesus!"

Perhaps the disciples are a gift for us because we can identify with the times they were not ready to understand the meaning of Jesus' words. We'd prefer to ignore certain passages of Scripture because the words are just too hard to put into action. Like the disciples, we have moments when we lack faith. If we had been "hanging out with Jesus," we, too, would probably have been terrified if the Risen Christ had come into the locked room where we were hiding out.

I do not fear to tread the path I cannot see Because the hand of One who loves is leading me.

Nyata

The previous days had been fraught with grief over the death of their beloved leader and tension that the Roman authorities might discover their relationship to Jesus. Would they take them away to be interrogated and then hang them on a cross? The men and women who had followed Jesus hardly knew which way to turn. They were talking about the supposed appearance of Jesus to two of their number. Had he really joined

On the Way to Emmaus *by Adrian Kupman*

them on the road to Emmaus? Had they truly recognized him in the breaking of the bread?

All these questions were churning in their minds when suddenly there he was. "Peace be with you," he said, but they felt far from peaceful. "They were startled and terrified, and thought that they were seeing a ghost." We understand such fear, for we have been fearful often ourselves. It wasn't until Jesus named their fear, their doubts, their lack of understanding that his voice began to sound familiar. When he instructed them to look at his wounded hands and feet, they recognized the wounds of love and knew that their beloved Jesus was with them again.

Why did Jesus come back? He knew these people and their needs. He understood their obvious fear, and he wanted to give them the gift of a peace that would last forever. His earthly presence had helped them feel secure; now he wanted them to feel his spirit even when his body was no longer present. Jesus had talked about peace before, but it was only in this context of true terror (would they be discovered?) that the disciples had a frame of reference that allowed them to put their whole faith in Jesus. Sometimes, we most keenly experience God's peace when we are in a time of trial.

I learned a great deal about strength of faith when they diagnosed my mother with inoperable cancer. Her longtime doctor's tears streamed down his face when he told her, "There comes a time in every human's life when medical science can do no more for them. Wanda, I'm sorry to tell you that time is here for you." After he and the rest of my family left the room, I asked my mother how she was feeling.

"I'm so glad I was raised in a Christian home," she responded. "God has been with me through all my life, and my faith in God is strong. God will see me through whatever is to come." Throughout the weeks until she died,

my mother's faith never wavered. God had sustained her through the deaths of her father, brother, and son. God would be with her until her earthly end. Her faith reminded everyone around her that, "Even though I walk through the darkest valley, I fear no evil; for you are with me" (Psalm 23:4).

Fear knocked at the door
Faith answered
No one was there.
Old English Legend

Think back to a time in your life when you felt fearful. Were you afraid of physical violence? Did you face a serious operation and wonder how it would turn out? Were there personal or financial problems that pressed in on you until you thought you couldn't breathe? What was your experience of God during this difficult time?

When I was in high school, a youth minister used an image that has stuck with me. He said that living in faith was like being on a huge ship with all of earth's people as inhabitants. The vessel was tossed and turned on gigantic waves that terrified many passengers. "Surely we will die!" they screamed. With every wave that crashed into the sides of the boat, some people cringed in terror. Others calmly waited for the storm to blow itself out. They were unaffected by the churning of the sea.

Why was it that some aboard the ship could be calm when others thought they would soon be dead? The ones at peace were those who believed in God; they realized that, though the boat tossed and turned in the storm, it was firmly anchored on a sandbar. No storm could capsize the ship; the sandbar of God's love kept it safely anchored.

I remember thinking how sad for those who screamed in terror. What joy for us who know that God's love surrounds us.

Moving Stormy Lives Toward Stability

It's dreadful when you feel like you are giving all that you have and getting nowhere. It's worse when you are also overcome with fear. How do you stop the horror?

The sea became rough because a strong wind
was blowing. When they had rowed about three or
four miles, they saw Jesus walking on the sea and
coming near the boat, and they were terrified. But he
said to them, "It is I; do not be afraid." Then they
wanted to take him into the boat, and immediately the
boat reached the land toward which they were going.

John 6:18–21

S ailing on the Sea of Galilee could be a very peaceful experience, almost boring. Still, because the conditions, especially the direction and briskness of the wind, can change rapidly, the boredom does not last very long.

Interestingly, several of the apostles whom Jesus had chosen were fishermen by trade. They had virtually grown up on the Sea of Galilee, sailing and casting their nets to try and make a catch, day after day, year after year.

Those fishermen would certainly be considered "expert" sailors, especially as far as the great lake of Galilee was concerned.

Certainly, their experience was a great advantage in navigating the large and fickle lake, which was also called Tiberias or Gennesaret.

However, just as today's highly trained meteorologists can make mistakes when forecasting weather, there was no way to know for sure what might happen to a boat when it was right in the middle of the Sea of Galilee.

That was especially true at night. In the dark, losing your sense of direction or progress was easy, especially if the sky was overcast. The fear factor related to the wind and the waves was also great.

That was what the apostles were up against when they set sail that evening from the eastern side of the Sea of Galilee. They were crossing to Capernaum, which was on the lake's northwest corner. After a long day of ministry, they were probably tired and anxious to get back home as soon as possible.

Where was Jesus in this picture? Nowhere, initially. Earlier in the day he had done a great miracle nearby, feeding a huge crowd with five loaves of bread and two fish. Afterward, Jesus had been beset by the crowds. As a result, he had withdrawn to the side of a nearby mountain to pray. As he left the site of the miracle, Jesus told the apostles to go on back to Capernaum without him.

As they went across the lake, the wind continued to pick up and the waves got bigger. Undoubtedly, their hearts were also beating faster and faster with the increasing danger. When they reached the middle of the lake, they weren't going anywhere in the strong wind.

Lord,
It sometimes seems like I'm swimming against the current, and I'm afraid of becoming exhausted and drowning. Please be with me and help me to get through the storm.
Amen

Suddenly, they saw a human figure coming toward them, walking on the water. Already anxious because of the conditions, they now became completely terrified! What really got to them was the totally unexpected sight

of Jesus, whom they had left behind at the base of the mountain, walking unhindered across the white-capped surface of the lake.

Can you imagine what that moment was like? John might have said something like, "Andrew, what is that over there?" Andrew's answer: "In all my years on this lake, I've never seen anything like it!" Then Peter might have cut in with: "I think it's Jesus! I can't believe it,... yes, it *is* Jesus, walking on water!"

Jesus immediately moved to calm a storm, but it was not the one raging on the lake. Rather, he sought to soothe the shattered nerves of his closest followers and friends, and he chose to do it in a unique way.

In other instances, Jesus moved to calm the circumstances. By doing so, he showed his divine power over nature. There could be no question that he was in control over even the most menacing conditions nature could create.

Here, though, Jesus did not choose to instantaneously bring the weather under control. Instead, right in the midst of the prevailing gusts, Jesus moved the boat several miles to shore in the virtual snap of a finger.

What insight this provides into one of the ways Jesus cares for his followers! In many cases, he allows us to struggle, to wait, to approach the furthest limits of our capacity. Then he moves in to make the decisive difference, and it happens so quickly that the outcome is almost a blur.

In such cases, Jesus does not cause the difficulties to go away. Instead, he takes us through the situation. It is like sitting in a traffic jam that is so congested your car does not move for hours. Then suddenly, though there are still many vehicles on the road, you find yourself going the speed limit for the rest of the trip.

In the end, understand that the Lord does not work in just one way. On occasion, he seems to do things in a way that reminds us he does not offer a singular, automatic response to our needs and prayers. He has our best interests in mind, and he chooses the way that will encourage the most growth in our lives. If we can keep that perspective, we are indeed on the path to the kind of wisdom Jesus wants us to gain and exercise.

From Fear to Peace

Jesus often spoke of peace and not being afraid. He wants to give us the gift of peace that casts out fear. Accept his gift.

❦

Peace I leave with you; my peace I give to you.
I do not give you as the world gives. Do not let your hearts
be troubled, and do not let them be afraid.

John 14:27

❦

This is not the first time we hear the counsel not to be afraid. Gabriel spoke these words to Mary when he announced that she would give birth to the Messiah. The angels spoke these words to the shepherds on the night of Jesus' birth. Jesus spoke these words to the disciples after his resurrection. In John 14, Jesus is preparing the disciples for his eventual departure from them. "Do not be afraid."

Despite his assurances, we are often afraid, and is it any wonder? The nightly news shows horrendous tales that inspire fear. We buy car alarms,

house alarm systems, and even guns. We worry about financial security, sinking money into insurance and investments. We lock the doors and windows. Our hearts are hardened toward strangers.

Most assuredly, we *should* be watchful and responsible in the care of our families. But fear is not cast out by locked doors. The peace of God releases fear. Jesus wants to give us peace, an assurance that no matter what happens we are not alone. The peace that Jesus gives is the quiet confidence that God is with us. Even when trouble strikes, God is present. God is at work in all things, working for good, working for justice, working for healing.

Each day we can take a moment to breathe in the presence of God. As we breathe in, we can say, "The peace of God is within me." As we breathe out, we can say, "The peace of God is all around me." This is not the peace of locked doors or big bank accounts. This is the deep peace of God that lets us walk through each day unafraid and knowing that God's peace can bear the day's troubles. Carry God's peace with you.

Every tomorrow has two handles. We can take hold of it with the handle of anxiety or the handle of faith.

Henry Ward Beecher

Confident of Spiritual Protection

The world in which we live is an increasingly dangerous place, with fewer and fewer exceptions as time passes. Can you ever really feel safe?

In the world you face persecution. But take courage;
I have conquered the world!

John 16:33

When you hear the word persecution, you tend to think of harassment, often violence. The reason is that religious persecution, such as the Holocaust or the more recent ethnic violence in Bosnia, is highly profiled. The number of deaths and the tragedy of starving prisoners catches the attention of many sensitive, caring people.

This may be the primary sense in which Jesus is referring to persecution. After all, Jesus and his disciples suffered ever more harassment until finally Jesus was crucified. Later, authorities intimidated the apostles, physically beat them, and, in several cases, killed them for their faith. Similar instances have taken place throughout the history of the Church.

The Crucifixion *by Jacopo Tintoretto*

Persecution is not always brought about by a group. It is far more common for persecution to take place one on one. When persecution is subtle, such as teasing or making fun of someone's beliefs, it is still difficult to stand up in such a situation because you feel like you are all alone.

Lord,
Even the thought of persecution creates
fear in my heart. But I thank you that I
can be encouraged, even courageous,
because you are in control.
Amen

If you believe in Jesus, who was brutally persecuted but was raised from the dead, you are never alone. He has conquered death and everything the world can throw at you. Take courage! You are on the winning team, forever and ever.

When Jesus Asks You Not to Judge

❧❧❧❧

Do not judge, so that you may not be judged.
For with the judgment you make you
will be judged, and the measure you give
will be the measure you get.

Matthew 7:1–2

Consequences and Judgment

When we refuse to become children of God, we experience consequences. First of all, the heart of Jesus breaks when we do not respond to his invitation. Then there are the rewards that we miss out on.

✦✦✦

Woe to you, Chorazin! Woe to you, Bethsaida!
For if the deeds of power done in you had been done in Tyre
and Sidon, they would have repented long ago in sackcloth
and ashes. But I tell you, on the day of judgment it will
be more tolerable for Tyre and Sidon than you.
Matthew 11:21–22

✦✦✦

The Greek word that is translated "woe" contains the notion of sorrowful pity and anger; thus the interpretation that Jesus shows anger resulting from a saddened heart. Chorazin's and Bethsaida's citzenry did not repent. Jesus says that two cities known for corruption—Tyre and Sidon—would certainly have changed their ways if they had witnessed the same miracles.

When Jesus began his public ministry, he called his listeners to change. "The time is fulfilled, and the kingdom of God has come near; repent, and believe in the good news" (Mark 1:15). He carried this message to cities and towns, from Galilee in the north to Jerusalem in the south. We do not know very much about Chorazin or Bethsaida, but Jesus stopped at both towns. The inhabitants heard his message, saw "deeds of power," and went

on their way. They did not respond nor change their ways. We do not know the evidence of their refusals, but we know that Jesus was troubled.

Have we also failed to respond to God's call? I think about the busyness of life, full calendars, active families, even active church life. We are often so busy and tired that when we stop to listen to God, we can be too weary to hear. Other times, when we do hear God, we choose not to respond or act. When we neglect what God leads us to do, are we really any different from the people of Chorazin or Bethsaida?

There are consequences to our decisions, just as we teach our children that there are consequences to their actions. If you touch the hot stove, you will get hurt. If you eat too much candy, you will not feel well. If you hit another child there will be a time out. Children learn cause and effect as it relates to behavior.

Jesus is saying there are consequences in refusing to repent, consequences that affect our daily life. We will miss out on the love, joy, and peace bestowed on his followers. We will not be a part of the community of faith, who hold each other accountable and offer guidance and assistance. We will not know the intimacy of prayer. We will feel the loneliness of the world. And we miss out on all of this because we are…too busy? Not interested? Too many other things to do first?

Loving God,
Open my eyes to your wonders: the magic of birds flying, the power of a sunrise, the glory of a blooming rose. I have witnessed your awesome deeds, and I want you to take my life and make it whole.
Amen

Jesus is passionately concerned about us. He wants us to know and follow God's way. He wants us to repent and change our ways. To experience the wholeness of life, life as God intended it, we must give ourselves over to him. Otherwise we miss out on God's precious gifts.

Remember that Jesus came into the world not to condemn us but to save us (John 3:16–17). He offered his life for us. God's judgment is tempered with mercy. Now is the perfect time to accept the good news of Christ!

Rocky Relationships

The illustration in Luke 12:57–58 drives home the point that we need to settle past accounts and disputes, and it is only common sense that we should try to live in harmony with others. How much more important that we be reconciled when our "accuser" or opponent is God!

And why do you not judge for yourselves what is right?
Thus, when you go with your accuser before a magistrate,
on the way make an effort to settle the case, or you may be
dragged before the judge, and the judge hand you over to
the officer, and the officer throw you in prison.

Luke 12:57–58

In any print media, such as advertising, magazine production, book publishing, and newspapers, there have always been battles between art directors and editors. The art staff constantly wants more space for art, and the editor constantly wants more space on the page for text. There is conflict on projects, and in the end, it seems as though our biases and opinions remain unchanged. Many art directors with whom I've worked are concrete thinkers, but most remain in the esoteric world of the creative thinker.

Editorial directors, like myself, are often visionaries who develop concepts we hope will be successful—not just in sales but in buyer impact. We stake our reputations on firm hunches and customer research. While we want to meet customers' needs, we often have our own agenda.

I don't mean to imply that no art directors are visionary abstract thinkers, or that editorial directors are never in touch with visual elements. Each side is driven by various energies—but it's only natural that tensions and disputes develop.

So when my boss resigned and an art director was promoted to vice president—and my boss—my heart sank. We already had a rocky relationship; he even tried to bar me from product development meetings. He seemed to view me as obstinate, and no doubt I was at times. On the other hand, he allowed his irritation with me to cloud the fact that I was a valuable asset to the company with much to contribute. It probably didn't help that he had publicly stated that he didn't want to work closely with a woman. How would he deal with me now that I reported directly to him? Aaagh!

I thought about my options:

Option #1—I could resign from my position and be free from the stress of working out a difficult relationship. Of course, my job would just be the first in a series of losses. Without my income, I would lose my car, my house, my computer (my only means of freelance income), and my self-esteem. I would be trading the freedom from daily stress at work for the anxiety of worrying about paying the bills at the end of the month.

. . . [F]or Jesus peace seems to have meant not the absence of struggle but the presence of love.
Frederick Buechner

Option #2—I could ask for a new supervisor, but that would probably mean a reassignment, a demotion, and a cut in pay. I didn't want to watch the projects I was so excited about fall through the cracks when I moved on. And a demotion would have felt like a surrender to his power tactics.

Option #3—I could stick it out and distance myself as much as possible from my new boss. Yet I still needed his approval for some of my projects, my

strategic five-year plan, my budget, and my
vacation. It would be impossible to dodge him
forever.

Option #4—I could negotiate for a new
relationship with him that was based on mutual
respect and a wipe-the-slate-clean approach. I could
compromise by forgetting that we had been
antagonistic peers and assure him that I would be a
supportive employee in spite of our combative
history.

A week after the announcement of his
promotion, I found myself summoned to my new boss's office. After he said a
few general things about the new directions in which he planned to take the
company, he asked me if I had anything to say.

The tension in my back was causing my head to throb as I raised my
white flag and laid out Option #4. I finished by telling the man that while we
had experienced some strained moments together and had our differences in
opinion, I hoped he and I would be willing to let go of the past and move
toward a more agreeable future.

I sat there relieved that I had done my best to make peace. My new
boss leaned back in his chair and said nothing for several minutes. Finally, he

grinned and, in an arrogant tone, said, "Well, I don't think you are capable of change, so we'll just have to see how things go."

That was not the response I had expected or hoped for.

Yet I walked out of his office knowing that I had chosen the right option. I had made the effort to settle my past accounts with this man. Sadly, he didn't seem to want reconciliation.

At first, I was angry and hurt by his comments. Later, a sense of peace came over me as I realized that I am capable of change. I could let go of my past with him. I would treat him with respect and be supportive... even if he was unable or unwilling to respond in the same way to me.

In Luke 12, Jesus suggests that we make every effort to settle disputes, quarrels, and controversies before it is too late. He does not promise, however,

that our efforts will always be rewarded with harmony and reconciliation. In this case, the effort I made to settle past accounts did not bring harmony, but I was provided with the peace of God that comes from choosing to obey his Word.

Judging Is Not up to Us

For some reason, we tend to evaluate other people. Are they good or bad? Stupid or smart? Rich or poor? Yet it's not our job to judge others. That remains the work of God. Our job is to love and accept others.

You judge by human standards; I judge no one. Yet even if I do judge, my judgment is valid; for it is not I alone who judge, but I and the Father who sent me.

John 8:15–16

Have you ever noticed how often we make snap judgments about people we hardly know? We catch a glimpse of a person and suddenly feel able to judge them by the words they speak, clothes they wear, company they keep. Most often, if we can take time to get to know that person, we realize that our first impressions were, at best, superficial; at worst, dead wrong. As a Russian proverb says, "When you meet a man, you judge him by his clothes; when you leave, you judge him by his heart."

Perhaps it is human nature to judge. Most people have at least a small core of insecurity that comes out in the need to compare. Is she smarter? Am I richer? Is my school better?

More insidious is our need to judge the heart and soul of another person. "She's only doing this to get ahead." "He's a stingy person." "She wouldn't offer help if it would save her life." "He's not a very ethical person." "I wouldn't trust him farther than I could throw him." "Have you ever met somebody so irresponsible?"

Jesus cuts to the chase on our need to stand in judgment of others. "You judge by human standards; I judge no one. Yet even if I do judge, my judgment is valid . . . ." In other words, our limited human experience does not give us the perspective or right to pass judgment on others. If judgment needs to happen, we can be sure that God will take care of it.

The next time you feel self-righteous judgment welling up inside you, try to catch yourself and analyze from where the need to judge is coming. Are you threatened by the other person? Feeling insecure about some aspect of your life? Do you need to stand out in the crowd? As the old adage says, "When you point the finger at somebody else, three fingers point back at you." Our need to judge usually says more about us than about the person we're judging.

When you feel the need to judge someone else, how about stopping to list five good qualities you notice about that person? If you can see their positive attributes, what you perceive as negative may not seem as important.

God calls us to love each other. This means being tolerant and accepting instead of intolerant and judgmental. Fortunately for us, God's spirit in us can help us make the leap from a negative thought to a positive thought. We can leave the complex job of judging to the One with a better perspective, and we can focus on loving acceptance.

Merciful God,
You love all of your children. You see the good in us all and help us grow to our full potential. Help me feel your love for me so that, when I am tempted to judge another person, I can remember that we are equal in your sight. Give me a heart so full of love and acceptance I have no need to be judgmental. Let me live in the spirit and name of Jesus Christ. Amen

A Different Approach

There really is a difference between our human nature and the nature of the divine. That difference is not restricted to the limitations of our talents and powers, but includes the varying ways we look at life and people.

❧❧❧

I do not judge anyone who hears my words and does not keep them, for I came not to judge the world, but to save the world.
John 12:47

❧❧❧

We know just how it should have been done. If *we* were God, we would *not* have done anything like this—it would be a much different and certainly better world.

We would have set clear rules. We would have said, "Obey these rules and salvation is yours; disobey and you will be judged accordingly." We would have established a list of 101 commandments. We would have established an action-centered, law-oriented, sin-conscious morality, with every word, thought, and action clearly designated as right or wrong.

And when people missed the point of why they were created—which was to obey us—they would have suffered. Judgment and punishment—that's how to get people's attention and teach them to behave. If those human beings were foolish enough to persist in their perverse ways, we could wipe them out

Jesus Christ

of existence. In fact, *we* might have avoided the frustrating situation entirely and never created humanity in the first place. One of the last things we would ever have considered doing was becoming human! Only someone much more loving than we would ever have done that.

Thankfully, we are not God. Our God does not give us lengthy lists of laws but rather fills holy pages with stories and parables that tell how God's mercy and love exceed human understanding. God does not focus on what we are doing but on the kind of persons we are becoming.

And when we have sinned, when we have disobeyed, does God cut us off? No! God forgives us, welcoming us back with open arms. God wants our fellowship, and to convince us of this expansive divine love, God even came to earth as one of us.

Our all-powerful Creator seeks not enforced obedience from us, but a relationship with us. For to be human is to be in relationship, and we are to be fully human. God has given us free will and then hopes for our freely given love! How incredible.

If you are pleased at finding faults, you are displeased at finding perfections.

Johann Kaspar Lavater

There is a giant chasm separating human judgment and divine judgment, and that chasm is filled with love. God comes to us, cares about us whether we consider ourselves worthy or not. The judgment we fear is a human-framed judgment made according to human standards. But it is God, in the person of Jesus, who says, "I came not to judge the world, but to save the world."

Jesus Urges Reconciliation

It doesn't matter who started the disagreement; Jesus says seeking reconciliation is more important than your obligation to worship.

❧❧❧

So when you are offering your gift at the altar,
if you remember that your brother or sister has
something against you, leave your gift there before
the altar and go; first be reconciled to your brother
or sister, and then come and offer your gift.

Matthew 5:23–24

❧❧❧

One Sunday, when my daughter was very young, she did something that resulted in a timeout for her and an angry feeling in me. I went to another part of the house to get ready for a trip to church. I was stewing about having to redo what I had already done, when I heard the sound of little feet on the wooden floor. Her timeout was not over but there she was with teary eyes wanting to reconnect with her father. She sought me out and helped me see the strength of our desire for reconciliation. We embraced, and I carry that valuable parable of reconciliation with me.

Worship was a sacred duty in the time of Jesus. For a Jew to be in a restored relationship with God, the appropriate sacrifice to God had to be made. Yet, as important as that relationship to God is, if you come to the altar while there is still enmity, Jesus advises that one should first go and be reconciled. Jesus is not overly concerned with who started the quarrel or disagreement, only that reconciliation is an obligation for the person of faith.

God of mercy,
You invite us into the ministry of
reconciliation. Give us the courage to take
the first step, to seek out others, to listen
to them, and to trust that you are present
working your will for reconciliation.
Amen

I remember incidents in our neighborhood when tempers would get heated in a teenage basketball game and an adult would step in and say, "Say you are sorry and shake hands." I never felt like doing that and often there would be a protest that it was the other person's fault. Yet the adult usually prevailed and something happened in that handshake that eased the confrontation. You cannot hit someone if you are holding their hand. The touch of flesh connects a child of God to a child of God. The basketball game

would go on, and I would be amazed at the gift of reconciliation.

As we grow older, we shift from adults guiding us in reconciliation to adopting that ministry ourselves. Paul says, "So if anyone is in Christ, there is a new creation: everything old has passed away; see, everything has become new! All this is from God, who reconciled us to himself through Christ, and has given us the ministry of reconciliation" (2 Corinthians 5:17–18). Now I am the adult teaching kids how to be reconciled when they disagree, and I still seek to resolve my own differences before going to worship.

The church can model reconciliation and practice reconciliation. In our society, we are too prone to get a lawyer. Many believe that nothing can be resolved except by the courts. We need to re-establish the practice of talking to one another, trusting God to lead us to reconciliation, developing skills in the church to resolve conflicts. The church can be a leader in teaching the art of negotiation, the blessings of listening, and the skills of conflict resolution.

The next time you receive communion, be conscious of someone you would want to take with you to the Lord's table. They may be people living or dead. Let that be the beginning of restoring relationships.

Clean Your Own House First

It's much easier to focus on other peoples' lives than to honestly appraise who we are and what we do. Jesus encourages us to get our own house in order before we start making judgments about other people.

❦

Why do you see the speck in your neighbor's eye, but do not notice the log in your own eye? Or how can you say to your neighbor, "Let me take the speck out of your eye," while the log is in your own eye? You hypocrite, first take the log out of your own eye, and then you will see clearly to take the speck out of your neighbor's eye.

Matthew 7:3–5

❦

I don't know about you, but I find my own faults much easier to understand than the faults of others. There are certain characteristics, qualities, and actions that in myself I hope are endearing, but when I encounter those same traits in others, I find myself annoyed!

Why is it that most of us can easily see the wrong that others do but are less perceptive when it comes to realistically looking at our own lives? When I make a mistake, I may have an explanation of why it happened. I was tired, I rationalize. Or, I didn't get enough help from other people. I made a mistake because I needed support. I wasn't given all the information.

"Let me take the speck out of your eye" (Matthew 7:4).

Because I see and understand things from my own perspective, my mistake may seem less important than someone else's error. Unable or unwilling to delve into another's experience, I judge them on what I see on the surface. Why did she mess up? There is no excuse! I can't believe he did that! I would never stoop so low.

Ah, but Jesus knows our game even though these thoughts may never be spoken out loud. As usual, Jesus understands our humanness but seeks to lift us to a higher level.

"You hypocrite, first take the log out of your own eye, and then you will see clearly to take the speck out of your neighbor's eye." When we hear

Jesus' comparison, we have to smile because we recognize that as easy as it is to see what's wrong with another person, it is harder to recognize and admit to our own mistakes. Better (but harder) to take care of our own "log" before we worry so much about our neighbor's "speck of dust."

Most people are like the Labrador spar crystal that appears dull and ordinary until turned around and viewed at a different angle. When the light strikes it just so, the Labrador spar crystal sparkles with brilliance. So with other people; we need to look at them from a variety of angles before we decide to judge who they are and why they do what they do.

Etty Hillesum was a young Jewish woman who lived in Amsterdam at the time of the Second World War. Her journals show not only what it was like for a Dutch Jew in those dark times but lets us share her spiritual struggles, as well. In *An Interrupted Life: The Diaries of Etty Hillesum,* she reminds us of our need to take an honest look at ourselves: "There is a really deep well inside me. And in it dwells God. Sometimes I am there too. But more often stones and grit block the well, and God is buried beneath. Then [God] must be dug out again."

Taking the "log" out of our own eye is the process of digging out God when the stones and grit of our thoughts, words, and actions get in the way

Instead of talking about other people's affairs, let me drive off my own wasps.

Japanese Proverb

of our relationship with the Holy One. We may not be ready to tell other people about the ways we "fall short of the glory of God," but until we openly converse with our Creator about our real lives, the well is clogged, the log still stuck.

To find a fault is easy; to do better may be difficult.
Plutarch

Confession creates a renewed relationship with God in which we see that we don't need to focus on other people's faults but rather we should take a close look at ourselves. Most of us would do well to start the day with quiet time in which we take stock of the previous day

and prepare ourselves to accept the new day as a present from God and live it well.

Here are some questions we might use in such a meditation: Was the spirit of Jesus evident in the way I lived yesterday? Do I regret any of my thoughts, words, or actions? Are there people with whom I need to make amends? Am I open to how God might use me today in his work? How can I live in harmony with all people this day? What special help do I need from God in the activities I have planned today?

What You Give Is What You Get

The Golden Rule, to "do unto others as you would have others do unto you," is almost universally recognized. But the Golden Rule is worded quite generally. What are some of its more specific implications?

Do not condemn, and you will not be condemned. Forgive, and you will be forgiven; give, and it will be given to you. A good measure, pressed down, shaken together, running over, will be put into your lap; for the measure you give will be the measure you get back.

Luke 6:37–38

"What you see is what you get" is almost a trademark saying of this generation. It sounds good, maybe even wise, to promote the concept of transparency in relationships.

Yet, looking at someone's personality and character, as important as that may be, is still only dealing with a limited dimension of life. Besides, the person who is opening up for inspection also needs to have some idea of what to expect in return for their transparency-based actions.

Jesus, of course, was the source of the Golden Rule. But he did not intend for it to be construed in terms of vague generalities. In other situations, Jesus spoke to closely related issues, making it clear that the Golden Rule is indeed distilled wisdom that when practiced yields rich dividends.

For example, Jesus draws out what is involved with condemnation and forgiveness. It is simple enough to say that if you don't condemn, you won't be condemned. The same goes for saying that if you forgive, you will be forgiven. Ho, hum.

Turn Jesus' sayings around, though, and you get an emotional baseball bat between the eyes! It's enough to cause you to break out in a cold sweat to think that if you condemn, you will also be condemned, or that if you don't forgive, you will not be forgiven. But that's the point. Thinking

through what Jesus is saying is an exercise in wisdom. It will give you pause before you choose to condemn someone or refuse to forgive a person who has wronged you.

Nor does Jesus stop there in working out the practical implications of the Golden Rule. He advises his hearers to give, that it may be given back. At first glance, the Golden Rule and these initial explanatory points, especially this one, may seem like a reciprocation principle. That is, it seems like a kind of spiritual pendulum swing effect: you give (it swings one way), you get (it swings back your way), and back and forth the same way every time.

In a general sense that is true, though our motive in giving should never be to get something back. Rather, the point is to assure you that the Lord will not let you become impoverished by virtue of how much you give.

But it is also an assurance that goes beyond that. The wording "a good measure, pressed down, shaken together, running over" is straight out of the marketplace in Jesus' day. A true full measure would be pressed down, shaken, and filled to the brim. If that were not done, you might end up being short-changed. In other words, Jesus' wording here is an elaborate description of getting your money's worth.

Obviously, this description speaks of going to significant length. That reflects the lengths God will go in making sure your giving to others will be responded to in full measure.

Lord,
I thank you for the assurance
that you not only forgive, but
that you also give back in
the measure we give, often
graciously even more.
Amen

Now that does not necessarily mean that the response will be "put in your lap" just as soon as you give to someone else. In fact, there is no promise anywhere in the Bible that you will be able to clearly discern when or how the full measure will be given back.

This is wisdom related to God's supernatural control of his created order. From a natural perspective, you give and it is gone. Hence, people seek tax breaks, favors in return, and the like. Otherwise, they usually feel that giving is pouring resources down the drain.

From the supernatural perspective of Jesus' words, however, you give, God uses it, and then returns it, somehow, in full measure. Thus, giving is anything but a waste. It is a wise spiritual and eternal "investment," since you can be sure that the Lord is managing this investment portfolio.

An Old Time-Saver

How do we make decisions about people, about events and beliefs, about our priorities, even about ourselves? Finding the "right judgment" to make these decisions can be quite a task.

Do not judge by appearances, but judge with right judgment.

John 7:24

These are busy days; we are all looking for ways to save time or energy. One time-saver that is as ancient as humanity itself is *prejudice*. Prejudice saves us time, since we don't have to investigate opinions, develop new friendships, or visit places or events. Prejudice eliminates the effort we might otherwise spend in mind-stretching learning or in acquiring innovative ways of looking at the world's problems or in understanding creative solutions to those problems.

The time that prejudice saves can be significant. Setting up a prejudice flowchart eliminates much hassle in decision making. We can differentiate

according to nationality or skin color, gender or age or size, religion or sexual orientation, school or workplace or residence, job or profession, dress or uniform or hairstyle, language or accent, size of family—there are many ways to use the prejudice time-saver. We need but be creative!

Placing every person, event, thought, or belief into a box, labeled and categorized, reduces the demands on our time. We can retain our same opinions throughout life and avoid messy transitions or ever having to change our position.

Of course, every efficiency device, including prejudice, does have a cost. As we use this time-saver, we bypass opportunities to learn and to develop interesting friends. Also, integrity and truth are part of the personal cost. The world loses the gifts and talents of those who are the casualties of those prejudices. And since prejudice is easily transmitted, the world moves that much further away from the possibility of peace, for God's inclusive, radical, all-encompassing love is again refused.

Ever-creating God,
In your boundless love
You are parent to us all.
How you must grieve
at the dissension among us,
your children.
Do you weep at what we do to one another?
Do you ever regret having created us?
We beg you—
Do not abandon us!
Help us see you in one another;
Remove from us our small-mindedness,
our prejudices and lack of vision.
Help us become what you created us to be—
One family,
United in your love forever.
Amen

No Room for Throwing Stones

"People who live in glass houses should not throw stones," goes the humorous saying. However, since almost everyone has significant shortcomings somewhere in their lives, shouldn't we all drop the rocks?

When they kept on questioning him, he straightened up and said to them, "Let anyone among you who is without sin be the first to throw a stone at her." And once again he bent down and wrote on the ground. When they heard it, they went away, one by one, beginning with the elders; and Jesus was left alone with the woman standing before him. Jesus straightened up and said to her, "Woman, where are they? Has no one condemned you?"

John 8:7–10

The word "hypocrite" comes from the Greek dramatic tradition of Jesus' era. It spoke of an actor who played a role and wore a mask that obscured his own features. Hence, the idea of "saying one thing and being another" that is usually attached to hypocrisy today.

The group that Jesus continually labeled as hypocrites were the Jewish religious leaders, notably the self-righteous Pharisees. He used strong descriptions of them like "whitewashed tombs," meaning attractive to the eye, but dead on the inside.

Certainly, there was no love lost between Jesus and these pompous leaders. He detested the total inconsistency between their religious image and their actual motives and behavior. They resented Jesus' appeal to the people, and they did everything they could to trick Jesus into some kind of mistake through which they could get rid of him.

This early morning encounter in the temple area was just such an attempt. Nothing is said about how this woman was caught in her adultery. However, it has all the earmarks of a setup, especially since there is no mention

Christ Reproving the Pharisees *by James J. Tissot*

of the man she was caught with, who was equally guilty.

The hypocritical religious leaders, the Pharisees, were testing Jesus, trying to force him to make a pronouncement opposing what the Law of Moses said about stoning adulterers or, at the very least, to make him look like a fool. But Jesus expertly turned the tables on them. The hypocrites ended up with egg all over their faces.

How did he do it? Jesus turned the spotlight from the accused to the accusers. He refused to focus on whether, morally, she should be stoned but rather on who is morally fit to do the stoning. Rather than stepping onto the trapdoor that had been set up for him, Jesus pulled the rug out from under the hypocrites who were conspiring to nail him.

Certainly, Jesus' brilliant question was much of what turned this difficult confrontation around. Since there was no denying that everyone in the crowd (except Jesus) had sinned, even the hypocrites were convicted in their consciences and had to back off from acting as if they were in the moral driver's seat.

Yet, it appears that there was also a key role in all this of Jesus writing on the ground. It is doubtful that Jesus was simply doodling in the dirt or merely playing mind games with the religions leaders.

There is no way to know for sure what he was writing. The most plausible explanation is that when Jesus bent down, he was writing out the Ten Commandments in the dirt. Certainly the command "You shall not commit adultery" was what was at issue when the woman was brought before Jesus. Yet other commandments, such as "You shall not bear false witness against your neighbor," also came into play, especially if catching this woman on this day was a full-blown setup. Whatever the case, the combination of Jesus' actions unnerved the attempted tricksters.

The wisdom of Jesus here relates to humility. None of us is in a position to be haughty in judging the actions of other people. That is not to say that there are not moral standards that must be guarded carefully if a society is to remain strong. It is to say, however, that no one except Jesus is in a position to make him or herself the standard. Very often, compassion is the better part of wisdom.

Lord,
Because I blow it so consistently,
I have to admit that I am in no
position to condemn anyone else.
Help me not to be hypocritical
but instead to be gracious to
those who fall short.
Amen

When Jesus Asks You to Be Merciful

Blessed be the God and Father of our Lord Jesus Christ, the Father of mercies and the God of all consolation, who consoles us in all our affliction, so that we may be able to console those who are in any affliction with the consolation with which we ourselves are consoled by God.

2 Corinthians 1:3–4

The Quality of Mercy

If mercy is the ability to have compassion and spare a person the consequences due him or her, then mercy is rare. Today, people seem more concerned with demanding justice than with mastering the Christlike quality of mercy.

Blessed are the merciful, for they will receive mercy.

Matthew 5:7

Mercy is the capacity to understand the feelings of someone who is hurting, despite that person's culpability in the circumstances. In the film based on her book, *Dead Man Walking,* the character of Sister Helen Prejean demonstrates the quality of mercy in many ways. The focus is on the relationship of a nun with a prison inmate convicted of rape and murder. It is a journey to search for redemption built on an admission of guilt, repentance, forgiveness, and mercy.

In his last days before execution, the convict shows no remorse, insisting he is a victim and attributing his crime to bad influences and substance abuse. But Sister Helen cares as much about saving the man's soul as saving his life. When he attempts to affix blame on everyone but himself, she insists that he admit his guilt and begin to feel regret. At the same time, she does everything in her power to extend mercy to the man, his family, and his victims' families. When she is unable to get the man's sentence changed to life imprisonment, she

The quality of mercy is not strain'd;
It droppeth as the gentle rain from heaven
Upon the place beneath: it is twice bless'd;
It blesseth him that gives and him that takes

           William Shakespeare, The Merchant of Venice

offers to stay with him through his execution.

At the end, the convict experiences God's mercy and forgiveness when Sister Helen refers to him as a "son of God," and he can look at her "face of love" as he enters death.

The merciful extend mercy to others, thus extending *God's* mercy to them. When we offer the "face of love" to one undeserving of mercy, have we not become Christlike? As we season justice with mercy, we help others to experience this part of God's character. In turn, we receive God's mercy and blessing.

The Vision of Peace

Peace will only come when we study it, pray for it, and work together to make it happen. The Bible calls us to be effective peacemakers. And while envisioning peace in today's world is difficult, if we do not make the first step, it will not happen at all.

Blessed are the peacemakers, for they will be called children of God.

Matthew 5:9

What is peace? Often, the peaceful reign of God is portrayed as an idyllic pastoral scene where people are engaged in endless repose. While occasionally we yearn for just such a calm existence, such a scene also prompts suspicions of boredom.

Of course, God's peace is far richer than that. Picture it as the real presence of God's love throughout the universe. Peace is not just calmness; it is a vibrant commingling of our humanity, talents, and gifts. It is the reflection

The Hebrew word shalom *is used today as a greeting in the Holy Land, just as we might use "hello" or "goodbye." Shalom, although often translated "peace," conveys much more than that. It is a vision, a promise, a prayer for health and healing and wholeness, for community, for freedom and justice.*

of the Spirit within each of us. Peace is unity glorying our diversity.

We often think of peace as a lack of disagreement. More specifically, it is the harmonious settlement of disagreements. When we respond to the struggles of others, offering them hope or a solution to their conflicts, we are working toward a far more encompassing peace than we may think.

Most of us believe that "charity begins at home." We hope that by doing good among our own, that goodness will spread out like concentric rings on the surface of a lake. And, if people pass their blessings along, that is true. Just for a moment, though, think of the lake water in reverse. Say you start from far outside your home and the circles travel inward to the core. Wouldn't that encourage you to also act more globally?

Our Mercy Comes From God

God is our model of unconditional love and mercy. That means our love must also be specific to everyone we meet. Even if we find it hard to love, God's love and mercy can flow through us to others.

But love your enemies, do good, and lend, expecting nothing in return. Your reward will be great, and you will be children of the Most High; for he is kind to the ungrateful and the wicked. Be merciful, just as your Father is merciful.

Luke 6:35–36

Because of their work hiding Jewish refugees, Corrie and Betsy ten Boom spent years in Ravensbruk, a Nazi concentration camp. Eventually, Betsy died there. After her release from the camp, Corrie ten Boom traveled around the world preaching a message of God's forgiveness. The strength of her belief was tested, though, when she met one of her former S.S. jailers at a Munich church where she had just preached.

Angel detail of Annunciation *by Bernardino Pintoricchio*

The sight of the jailer awaked ten Boom's painful memories of the camp. When he came forward to shake her hand, she was stunned to hear him say that Jesus had died for his sins also! Corrie ten Boom was unable to lift her hand to meet his. She couldn't even manage a smile. So she prayed for Jesus to forgive her and for help to forgive the man. She was still unable to respond. When she prayed that she could not forgive him, and she asked only for forgiveness for herself, she felt a current of love shoot down her arm toward the man she had every reason to hate.

Those who look for reasons to hate miss opportunities to love.

Carmen Sylva

There may be times in our lives when we need God's love and mercy to take over where our own fail. The good news is that

*Although he hates me,
if I do not hate him
enmity will soon be at an end.*
        Chinese proverb

not only did God show us how to love, God's love is available to us to share with others. As Saint Catherine of Siena said, "The only thing we can offer to God of value is to give our love to people as unworthy of it as we are of God's love."

Que Huong and her husband, Ngoc Phuong, lived quietly in their Vietnamese village until they found themselves caught between the opposing forces of their country's civil war. Not wanting to join either the revolutionary forces or the armies of the Thieu government, Huong and Phuong participated in a peace march for which they were arrested and thrown into prison. They were beaten and tortured, and finally, Phuong died.

When Que Huong was released from prison at the end of the war, she was asked what she would do if she met the man who had tortured her and Phuong in prison. The gentle woman replied that she still held the "flame of anger" inside her, but she knew that

killing her torturer would cause his family to take revenge on her. She wants the hatred to stop.

Throughout history, there have been persons who have shown love when hate would have been understandable. We are amazed when we see the ability to love even in the face of personal pain and loss, the capability to show mercy even when revenge would be a natural response. Could we manage the same forgiveness? Does

But now in Christ Jesus you who once were far off have been brought near by the blood of Christ. For he is our peace; in his flesh he has made both groups into one and has broken down the dividing wall, that is, the hostility between us.

Ephesians 2:13–14

our mercy reach that far? We know that even though we try to live in love, we will have times of feeling angry, hurt, eager for revenge.

Fortunately, God has given us the highest example of mercy: He sent his beloved son, Jesus, for our sakes. God enables us to begin each new day feeling loved and forgiven. And because we saw in Jesus one who could confront injustice without hating the unjust, we know that such love is possible, even for us.

As Generous as Jesus

The most generous gift we have ever received was Jesus Christ; through his example we are encouraged to find our own ways to be generous.

*In all this I have given you an example that
by such work we must support the weak, remembering
the words of the Lord Jesus, for he himself said,
"It is more blessed to give than to receive."*

Acts 20:35

This verse in Acts is not found in the four gospels. Nevertheless, it rings true as the Jesus we have met through Matthew, Mark, Luke, and John. The Jesus of the gospels was generous with his time. He sat with the woman at the well and led her to a new understanding of herself (John 4). He had time to hold children on his lap and bless them, despite the attempts of the disciples to move them along (Mark 10:13–16). He would interrupt his travels to respond to those in need of healing, as with blind Bartimaeus

Jesus and the woman at the well

(Mark 10:46–52). Jesus was generous, even with those whom others shunned.

Jesus taught the crowd on the hill, using easily understood parables based on their daily lives (Matthew 5). In the midst of his Sabbath teaching in the synagogue, he touched and healed a woman who had been bent over for 18 years (Luke 13:10–13). Jesus was generous with his words and his miraculous touch.

We usually think that generosity only involves money. Yet, Jesus would prefer we show our generosity through service. A good way to practice generosity is by doing a private act of kindness or performing an unseen service. Practice giving that does not benefit you—we do not give in order to receive. Send a note of appreciation to someone who does not get much recognition. Do the dishes even if it isn't your turn. Pay for the car behind you at a toll both. Deliver a plant to a church secretary. Throw a surprise party for a friend.

Teach us, good Lord, to serve Thee as Thou deservest:
To give and not to count the cost…
To labour and ask for any reward
Save that of knowing that we do Thy will.
                              St. Ignatius Loyola

Paul says that generosity is one of the fruits of the Spirit (Galatians 5:22). Generosity flows from the heart, from the abiding trust that God is at work. God is a God of abundance, and what we give away does not diminish us but clears out more room for God to be generous to us. The more we trust God in our giving, the more thankful our hearts become in seeing that everything is a gift from God. If we have freely received, then we may also freely give.

Not long ago, our church held a drive for families in another state that had been hit by devastating fires. Our community had also experienced fires, so there was a generous response. A couple of weeks later there was another fire, and a family from our church was burned out. They appeared in worship the next Sunday to thank the church for support, to testify that they were going to survive, and to announce that the only things intact were those set aside for our campaign for the fire victims. They taught us about thankfulness and generosity that day.

Sermon on the Mount *by James J. Tissot*

An old African proverb says, "it is the heart that gives, the hand that lets go." Pray that you might have a generous heart and enjoy finding all the ways you can give.

The Balm of Forgiveness

Jesus is not implying that God's forgiveness for our sins is dependent on our forgiveness of others. Rather, he says that walking in fellowship with God is impossible when we refuse to forgive others. Our ability to forgive others can be broadened when we realize that *we* have been forgiven.

For if you forgive others their trespasses, your heavenly Father will also forgive you; but if you do not forgive others, neither will your Father forgive your trespasses.

Matthew 6:14–15

For 18 years my husband and I worked with junior and senior high students in a youth ministry program at a small church. In spite of a few occasional struggles over philosophy and budget, we always sensed the congregation's support and felt at home there. In the middle of our 18th year, we began to feel a sense of restlessness and a desire to rest or take a sabbatical. As we resigned from our positions, we felt confident that we would be deeply missed. However, some reactions to our resignation proved surprising—and painful.

Just prior to our departure, the church took a survey regarding ministries of the church. Some church members apparently felt that they  should not pay us for our 30-plus hours a week since other ministry leaders "volunteered out of the goodness of their hearts." Some people wrote in questions such as: "Why is the youth budget so much larger than the children's ministry budget?" and "Why should the church focus so much effort and money on reaching out to students whose families aren't involved in our church?"

My heart was broken. After so many years of trying to help church members see the value of investing time, money, and ministry in the mission field on our doorsteps, some of them still didn't get it! And then to question our integrity, our motives, and our stewardship—I didn't feel much like forgiving.

As we met for the last time with the congregation, we broached these issues and invited those who had problems with our ministry to privately discuss the topics. When no one came forward, the anger inside me began to layer itself. This was not how I wanted to feel about our departure. How could

I rid myself of anger and frustration when the persons who had written the remarks refused to step forward? My stomach was in knots, and I felt bitterness gaining its grasp on my soul.

Then it came to me. What a hypocrite I am! How can I ask God to forgive me for my shortcomings if I am not willing to forgive those who have hurt me? Clearly, our critics at the church did not have the full picture of our ministry and were speaking from uninformed perspectives. They didn't know the level of our financial commitment, or that many students with whom we worked had no other Christian influence outside the youth ministry.

Instead of complaining to God about these people, I needed to pray that God would make the emotional, spiritual, physical, and financial needs of those students real in the hearts of our critics, that one or more volunteers would step up to fill our shoes in the youth programs, and that the church as a whole would consider students from unchurched homes a fertile mission field.

Forgiveness is the economy of the heart. . . . Forgiveness saves expense of anger, the cost of hatred, the waste of spirits.

Hannah Moore, Practical Piety

How difficult—but necessary—it is to surrender our grievances and grudges to God! Denying forgiveness to others is selfish *and* self-destructive. But when we release our bitterness before God, we will find balm, liberation, and forgiveness for others *and* for ourselves.

Why Forgive?

As long as we deny forgiveness to others, we deny ourselves healing. Each retelling of an injury removes the delicate scar tissue slowly forming over our pain and our bleeding begins again. Each remembrance renews the injury.

❦

Then Peter came and said to him, "Lord, if another member of the church sins against me, how often should I forgive? As many as seven times?" Jesus said to him, "Not seven times, but, I tell you, seventy-seven times."

Matthew 18:21–22

❦

Our immediate response in the aftermath of injustice, cruelty, betrayal, neglect, or abuse is often refusal to forgive. The act is too recent; we are in shock; we cannot forgive.

For a time we must go over what was done, enter into the pain, while gently embracing our shattered core. Carefully, fearfully, we assess the damage done to us. Eventually, we encounter the question of forgiveness.

And though our feelings and beliefs concerning forgiveness are in the spiritual and emotional realm, we describe the situation using terms and metaphors from the physical realm. We talk of being wounded, of hurting, of breaking hearts, of seeking or desiring healing, of bearing scars. We describe each reminder of the act as a reopening of the wound.

As time passes, we may come to the conclusion that those who injured us do not deserve forgiveness; there may even be an absence of sorrow or remorse on the part of those guilty. Yet, forgiveness is not dependent upon an

admission of either guilt or sorrow; nor does forgiveness always reduce the hurt or injustice committed.

We, the wounded, have become the one who is bound and held hostage to our experience.

Only forgiveness can undo those ties binding us to the past. Only forgiveness frees us for the life that we cannot fully experience until we have released the hurting.

It may be that we cannot forgive from our own strength and mercy. It may be that the starting point of our forgiveness is to immerse ourselves in God's forgiveness. Within God's unlimited love is found the mercy we lack. When we allow that divine flood of mercy to wash over us, it can cleanse us from bitterness and thoughts of vengeance. And then, enveloped in God's boundless love, the river of God's mercy flows both to us and to those who injured us. That is when our scars become our victory badges!

Counting the numbers has always been a human propensity. We continue to live and to judge and to extend or withhold forgiveness according to the numbers. We measure a church's success by the size of its congregation. We evaluate Bible study programs and prayer meetings by the numbers attending. By focusing on numbers, we rapidly lose the vision of God's loving kindness and generosity and mercy.

Forgiveness Flows

Forgiveness for our sins or for someone who has sinned against us releases God's power to flow to us and those around us. Forgiveness is a dynamic of our merciful God.

※※※

Forgive us our sins, for we ourselves forgive everyone indebted to us.

Luke 11:4

※※※

A friend of mine rewrote the Lord's prayer in contemporary verse. I don't know if he started from the original Greek, but his version touched me. He said, "Let forgiveness flow from each one, to each one, to each one." The first time I prayed that, the addition of the third phrase struck me. It was so true. Forgiveness should flow and keep on flowing from each one, to each one, to each one. There is a dynamic at work in forgiveness. It starts a chain reaction. As we let go of the sins against us, it releases others who are also bound by past hurts and wounds.

It starts with recognition of our own need for forgiveness. A harsh word, an intentional rejection, a forgotten appointment are not only breaks in our relationships, but they also affect our relationship with God. Early Christians understood this. When Jesus invites us to pray that our sins be forgiven, it is a step toward making amends with those we have harmed or offended. The forgiveness of God releases an energy in us to make peace with others.

At the end of World War II, twenty thousand German war prisoners were marched through Russia toward their country. As they entered Moscow, people lined the streets to look and to jeer at the generals strutting with their heads high in an attitude of superiority. Next came the German soldiers, weary and worn, bandaged and hobbling, heads bent down. An elderly woman in the crowd pushed her way through the police cordon and ran toward a soldier with a crust of bread for the hungry enemy. It released something in the crowd, and soon others offered a drink or piece of food as the soldiers marched along. There was still anger, but there was a deeper sense of recognition that each German soldier was some mother's son.

It was a step toward forgiveness. One woman's act created a new possibility, set loose a new wave of forgiveness and compassion.

Any rabbi with a group of disciples would teach them a way to pray. We have been blessed with this prayer of Jesus and we are encouraged to make forgiveness a part of our prayer and part of our life. Forgiveness opens a path, clears a blocked stream so that we may be fully alive and in harmony with others. As we forgive others, we can discover the courage to forgive ourselves.

Are you holding on to another person's error? Can you ask God for forgiveness for your errors and also for others? Are you willing to let go of the burden of anger and resentment, guilt and recrimination, and move into the freedom of God's forgiveness?

WHAT A FRIEND WE HAVE IN JESUS

What a friend we have in Jesus, all our sins and griefs to bear!
What a privilege to carry everything to God in prayer!
O what peace we often forfeit, O what needless pain we bear,
all because we do not carry everything to God in prayer.

Joseph Scriven

Once More With Feeling

All of us stumble and fall occasionally, even in our spiritual lives. Jesus reminds us that whenever we make mistakes, we can repent and begin again. On the other side, we are also called to forgive others every time they offer repentance. Sometimes that's harder!

If another disciple sins, you must rebuke the offender, and if there is repentance, you must forgive. And if the same person sins against you seven times a day, and turns back to you seven times and says, "I repent," you must forgive.

Luke 17:3–4

Fred was an active member of his local church. On Sundays, his fellow members saw him as a jovial, outgoing man, always ready to lend a hand. So when he first asked for a loan from another member—"Just a few dollars to tide me over"—nothing was made of it. One loan led to another, though, until Fred owed money—lots of it—to almost everyone in the church. Fred's compulsive gambling finally became known when his inability to pay back his loans led to one woman's own financial problems.

"I'm truly sorry," Fred announced to person after person as he explained his problem. Each lender understood, forgave him, and hoped he would get over his problem. The pattern repeated, however, as Fred's addiction overcame his desire to begin again. As hard as it was, the church members continued to forgive and love Fred, though they finally realized that loaning him money was not the loving thing to do since it enabled him to continue his destructive behavior.

Instead, after the repentance and forgiveness scenario had played out many times, some members gathered with Fred to talk honestly about his gambling compulsion. "You need help, Fred. This is not something you can lick by yourself," one woman said. "Give it to God, Fred," another person suggested, "and join a twelve-step group so that you have a support system to maintain a healthy way of being." The woman whose own finances

"I can forgive, but I cannot forget," is only another way of saying, "I will not forgive." Forgiveness ought to be like a canceled note— torn in two, and burned up, so that it can never be shown against one.

Henry Ward Beecher

were in jeopardy because of her loans to Fred took a deep breath, looked Fred in the eye, and said, "I will go with you to your first few meetings. I want to try to understand what your addiction is like."

Fred found a group for recovering gamblers where he heard many stories similar to his: persons struggling with addiction who were occasionally overwhelmed by it, acted hurtfully toward others, repented, and asked for forgiveness. Not everyone had been as fortunate, though, to have a loving community who shared God's mercy by offering forgiveness and holding the gambler accountable for his or her actions.

This church community took seriously Jesus' words: "If the same person sins against you seven times a day, and turns back to you seven times and says, 'I repent,' you must forgive." With addiction, though, they realized that mercy and forgiveness also meant helping the addict toward wholeness. Their money didn't help Fred live as a person of God; their forgiveness and support did help usher him into a new period of his life.

Forgiveness, No Matter What!

Prisoners of war and others who have suffered greatly for long periods often have a tremendously hard time forgiving those who have caused the pain. What should you do when forgiveness is so difficult?

When they came to the place that is called The Skull, they crucified Jesus there with the criminals, one on his right and one on his left. Then Jesus said, "Father, forgive them; for they do not know what they are doing." And they cast lots to divide his clothing.

Luke 23:33–34

Forgiveness, as a concept, is easy to understand. It means to grant pardon for an offense. It also usually includes releasing resentment against the person who committed the offense.

However, as easy as the *idea* of forgiveness is to comprehend, it is anything but easy to *do*. It is true that if the offending act is relatively small, forgiveness may come more easily. But that is usually because there was also very little offense taken.

Christ Falls on the Road to Calvary *by Raphael*

Whenever there is much riding on the offense, the accompanying emotions of anger and resentment usually become dramatically harder to defuse. In addition, it is easy to convince yourself that what you feel is reasonable. It seems as if it is your inalienable right to hold onto the rage.

As he died in excruciating pain on the cross, Jesus had much to resent. The envious and paranoid religious leaders had stalked him at length, arrested him on a trumped-up charge, forced him to undergo the injustice of a "kangaroo court," and sentenced him to death. He was then brutally beaten before being made to carry his own cross to the hill where the death sentence would be carried out—in the company of two hardened criminals.

Truly, it was a horrible death! Crucifixion produced intense suffering. First, driving nails through the hands and feet attached the person's body to the cross. Beside the unending, searing pain of those wounds, the weight of the body pulled the limbs out of joint. That made it extremely difficult to breathe and caused the internal organs to begin to collapse on each other. In the end, most died of asphyxiation.

So then, putting away falsehood, let all of us speak the truth to our neighbors, for we are members of one another. Be angry but do not sin.... Put away from you all bitterness and wrath and anger and wrangling and slander, together with all malice, and be kind to one another, tenderhearted, forgiving one another, as God in Christ has forgiven you.

Ephesians 4:25–32

Roman citizens did not usually experience this cruel and lingering form of death. It was a symbol of brute power of the ruling class over the masses.

Yes, Jesus had plenty to resent, if he chose to do so. But he did not. Rather, as he hung on that hideous cross, he was primarily concerned with exactly the opposite: forgiveness. He asked his heavenly Father to forgive the

very people who had unjustly done this to him.

How do you know if you have forgiven? Many believe that you have not really forgiven until you have forgotten the offending act. If the incident repeatedly comes to mind, it is evidence that you have not fully forgiven. The error in this thinking, though, is that, in forgetting, we would never learn from what happened.

Forgetting something that is painfully vivid requires an active "erasing" of the memory. Rarely it may happen through amnesia or brain damage. However, *forcing* yourself to forget is repressing or blocking the memory, and that's a very unhealthy thing to do.

If anything, true forgiveness requires remembering, at least until you've truly forgiven. You have to remember what happened in order to come to grips with your strong negative feelings. Forgiveness becomes the choice to release the powerful emotions involved. Don't be discouraged if that choice has to be made repeatedly before your emotions are laid to rest.

It is important to remember one other thing related to forgiveness. From the cross, Jesus said: "Father, forgive them, for they do not know what they are doing." As hard as it may be to fathom, sometimes one person can be grievously hurt by someone else's actions or words without that other person knowing. At other times, as with Jesus, those involved knew their actions were serious. Yet, they had absolutely no idea how serious. They had executed Jesus, the Son of God, who was completely innocent of any of the charges leveled against him.

Jesus' example is sound, even if our emotions don't agree. If he could forgive, given what was done to him, we must at least realize it is important to follow suit.

Forgiveness can be a long and bumpy process, but it is worth it. If you stubbornly refuse to forgive, it is not so much the person or persons you refuse to forgive who are hurt. You are being eaten up inside by the resentment you refuse to release. The person you should have forgiven likely has no clue what you are feeling. Thus, if you don't forgive, all your precious emotional energy is being wasted just as much as if you flushed it down the garbage disposal.

Lord,
I have trouble forgiving. I secretly prefer to hang on to resentment. Help me to make the choice to forgive, even if it has to be made repeatedly.
Amen

Mercy Matters More Than Appearances

"Going through the motions" means you are doing something that should be done but your heart is not in it. Is it the action or the motivation that counts?

Go and learn what this means, "I desire mercy, not sacrifice."
For I have come to call not the righteous but sinners.

Matthew 9:13

Apparently, instances of carrying through an action "for the sake of appearance" are at least as ancient as the time of Jesus. The Pharisees, a group of religious leaders of Jesus' day, desperately wanted to look righteous in the eyes of the people. As a result, they simply could not understand why Jesus chose the opposite stance.

When you do things for the sake of appearance, you strive to be at the right place, at the right time, with, of course, the right people. That means, often, that the sole reason you make an appearance at certain events is to look good.

Sadly, throughout history, this has happened with many people regarding worship. Whether it is the giving of a special sacrifice, some earmarked offering, a high-profile pledge, or simply attendance at a spotlighted service, some get involved primarily for the sake of appearance.

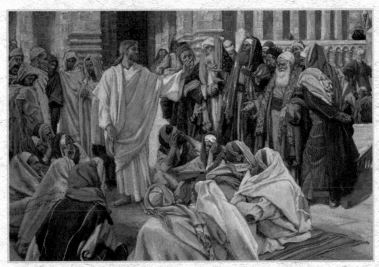

Such appearances, especially those that are finely tuned, may impress a great many people. They will think well of you. They may even admire you . . . or, at least the "you" they think you are. Perhaps there is something to be said for going through the motions in

Pharisees Question Jesus *by James J. Tissot*

such religious observances. After all, you came, you gave, you were useful. Some people don't even get that close.

On the other hand, we have Jesus. He always seemed to be at the wrong place at the wrong time . . . usually with the wrong people—at least from the Pharisees' perspective. For example, the Jews utterly despised Roman tax collectors. They were more feared than the IRS is today. Thus, the Pharisees could not imagine why Jesus would be seen with such riffraff. But, in his presence, the tax collectors were deeply conscious of their sin.

Lord,
Help me not to focus on how I look on the outside, but how I really am on the inside. And, just as I need your mercy, help me to be merciful to others in need.
Amen

What the Pharisees overlooked was Jesus' motivation. He did not minister based on appearance—an idea that was totally foreign to them. His choices were to actually *do* good. When quizzed about his relationship with such rabble, Jesus answered using a powerful analogy. "Doctors don't spend time with those who are well, but with those who are sick!"

Of course, the Pharisees were "sick" too. They just didn't know it. They were religious, but they weren't really "righteous"— just self-righteous. They had the appearances and images down pat, but not the reality. They showed no mercy and, thus, received none in return.

The lesson here is that Jesus has mercy on those who acknowledge their shortcomings. We need his mercy far more than we need to be seen as righteous. And we need to be much more merciful to others rather than being absorbed with our own needs.

Tell Others About God's Mercy!

"Word of mouth" is the way satisfied customers pass on their sense of appreciation. If we are willing to tell others about some relatively unimportant product, what about telling them about God's incredible mercy?

As he was getting into the boat, the man who had been possessed by demons begged him that he might be with him. But Jesus refused, and said to him, "Go home to your friends, and tell them how much the Lord has done for you, and what mercy he has shown you." And he went away and began to proclaim in the Decapolis how much Jesus had done for him.

Mark 5:18–20

D ave Dravecky was a good major-league baseball player who is better known for how his baseball career ended. While pitching for the San Francisco Giants, Dravecky found out he had cancer in his left arm—his throwing arm.

The amazing thing about Dave Dravecky was that, after surgery and extensive therapy, he was able to make a comeback and pitch again in the major leagues. The sad end to that gutsy comeback came when, during a widely watched telecast, there was a "pop" like a gunshot from Dravecky's throwing arm as he delivered a pitch.

The bone in the arm, weakened by cancer therapy, had snapped like a dry, slender branch. Dave Dravecky would never pitch again. In fact, additional surgery proved necessary and they removed the entire arm and shoulder to make sure all the cancerous tissue was gone.

Lord,
Open my eyes to your
mercy in my life. Also,
show me the situations
in which I can share
that appreciation with
those who need to hear.
Amen

Was Dave Dravecky bitter? No. He was deeply disappointed, but he knew that it was only because of God's mercy that he was still alive and had been given the opportunity to defy all odds and pitch again at the major-league level.

What has Dave Dravecky done since the dramatic end to his baseball career? To a large extent, he has been telling other people about God's grace and mercy. Yes, Dravecky's book about his experience and his many public and church speaking engagements begin with his baseball career and his bout with cancer. But they climax with his testimony about what the Lord has done in his life.

There is a very real sense in which the man Jesus healed was an ancient Dave Dravecky. Certainly, his healing was more dramatic than Dravecky's. Yet, like the baseball player, his notoriety gave him the opportunity to tell many people what had happened to him and how God had mercifully acted on his behalf.

Much like Dave Dravecky, the man who experienced Jesus' healing touch did not hesitate to seize the opportunities placed before him. He moved throughout his home region, joyfully telling of the mercy of the Lord.

How much are you like Dave Dravecky? Consider this: In one way or another, we all owe a great deal to God's mercy in our lives. Because that is true, isn't it the wisdom of Jesus for you to also express your appreciation to those around you?

When Jesus Asks You to Be Humble

Whoever becomes humble like this child is the greatest in the kingdom of heaven.

Matthew 18:4

Realistic Humble Confidence

When some people go fishing, they expect the fish to jump in the boat. When that doesn't happen, they give up quickly. What can you learn from impatient fishermen that is of eternal significance?

As he walked by the Sea of Galilee, he saw two brothers, Simon, who is called Peter, and Andrew his brother, casting a net into the sea—for they were fishermen. And he said to them, "Follow me, and I will make you fish for people." Immediately they left their nets and followed him.

Matthew 4:18–20

Fishing can be an exercise in frustration, especially if your ego is on the line. If your expectations are too high, if you have bragged about how many fish you will catch, or about how big the fish you catch will be, the trip can turn out to be a meal of humble pie. It is different when you fish for a living...*if* you are going to make a living at fishing. The cocky and shortsighted don't last long as professional fishermen. They can't take the waiting and humbling.

On the other hand, there is a special kind of confidence that effective fishers possess. Even though they know that many factors impact the fishing, they also know that alertness, shrewdness, and perseverance usually pay off in the end. Over time, the large catches will be made, though sometimes in ways you don't expect.

Several of Jesus' closest followers, including Simon Peter and his brother, Andrew, were veteran fishermen. From long experience, they understood the patience and humility it takes to land fish. They did not comprehend, however, how to land a person by telling them about Jesus. They possessed neither the patience nor the humble confidence needed to be effective in that realm.

Jesus had watched them fish. He realized that fishing, in many respects, is like witnessing to other people. But the disciples didn't understand that. So while they possessed the proper humble confidence for fishing, they had no experience in telling others about Jesus. They tended to be either fearful or falsely confident. That seems to be why Jesus worded his call to Peter and Andrew the way he did. He knew that, in asking them to move from all they had ever known to the unknown, any parallels to fishing would make the call less fearful for them.

Lord,
Help me to develop the kind
of healthy humility that is a
basis for an effective life.
Amen

Fishing for people was indeed a perfect illustration for fishermen to relate to talking to people. Peter and Andrew were much more comfortable in dealing with fish than people. But things would change for the better. The same alert patience that made them successful fishermen also made them highly effective fishers of people.

As apostles, Peter and Andrew, plus the other professional fishermen James and John, saw thousands of people respond in faith as they shared their own faith in Jesus. They "reeled them in" with the same kind of humble, patient confidence with which they had fished the Sea of Galilee.

The rapid response of Simon and Andrew reveals a great deal about how they felt about future success. They left with Jesus immediately, not because they hated fishing, but because they knew that fishing for people was the wise way to invest the humble confidence they had learned.

Bigger Starts Smaller... and Grows

Much of our society is committed to a bigger is better philosophy. But with the focus on bigger, we tend to forget that bigger usually started smaller. How do we get a balanced perspective on the beginning of bigness?

He put before them another parable: "The kingdom
of heaven is like a mustard seed that someone took
and sowed in his field; it is the smallest of all the
seeds, but when it has grown it is the greatest
of shrubs and becomes a tree, so that the birds of
the air come and make nests in its branches."
Matthew 13:31–32

Not everyone can work up the nerve to attend their tenth anniversary high school class reunion. But if you do, you will probably agree that there are two interesting trends. You see the early faders and the late bloomers.

Early faders are the people who topped out in high school or shortly thereafter. They were the ones who were unusually physically mature for the school years. Often, they were very attractive and considered among the coolest kids in school. And, back then, you tended to think things would always be that way.

Time marches on, though, and time can make a world of difference with the early faders. Full heads of hair and muscular physiques can give way to baldness and potbellies. The most beautiful female faces and figures can fill out from childbirth or weight gain.

It may come as a shock that many of the beautiful people that you remember aren't any more by that fateful tenth reunion. Not only that, but most of those you thought of as big and scary aren't either. What happened?

You grew! They didn't get any smaller; you got bigger. That prepares you for the second trend, the late bloomers.

At the reunion, it may seem like there has been an invasion of people you never met before. And, in a sense, that is true. Some of those you went to high school with had not physically and emotionally developed into the people they have become. You may remember them as small, awkward, and unsure. Ten years later and after a major growth spurt, there is a polish and a confidence that was not there before.

Again, the subconscious thought that "Things will always be this way" is proven wrong! How someone, or something, starts may not provide a accurate idea of how things will turn out.

Take Michael Jordan, for example. His long-time exploits in winning N.B.A. scoring titles and world championships with the Chicago Bulls cause us to forget his humble beginning as a basketball player. Long before he was an All-American at the University of North Carolina or an N.B.A. superstar, Jordan was cut from his high school basketball team.

Not making the basketball squad would be humiliating for anyone. It may seem ironic from this vantage point, but there was a time when it

Lord,
I want to be part of your
kingdom and its growth. I
ask that you take the tiny
mustard seed of my faith
and cause it to flourish and
bless the lives of others.
Amen

certainly appeared unlikely that Michael Jordan would become one of the greatest basketball players who ever lived.

Another classic example is the artist Grandma Moses. For what would be an entire career for most people, Grandma Moses worked embroidering on canvas. Then, in her midseventies, her hands became arthritic, and she was unable to hold the embroidery needles.

So, from the memories of her childhood in the late 1800s, Grandma Moses began to paint at age 76. Despite never having an art lesson, within three years her work was included in a major show at the Museum of Modern Art in New York City. She continued this astounding late-found painting career and had worldwide acclaim until near her death, when she was over 100 years old.

So beware of basing wider expectations on humble present-tense appearances. Things often turn out dramatically different than they start. There may end up being a lot more present than the seemingly limited potential you thought was there.

This is the point Jesus was making about the growth of the kingdom of heaven. Like a very small seed sowed, unnoticed, in a field, the outworking of God's kingdom on earth had a humble beginning with Jesus and a few followers. But that was not the end of the story; it was hardly the beginning.

That small seed in Jesus' story may not have been noticed for some time. But it soon made itself known as it began to grow. Eventually, it grew into a tree large enough for birds to nest in its branches.

Similarly, the kingdom of God (or heaven, since the terms were used interchangeably) has grown by leaps and bounds. From a spiritual standpoint, like the tree of Jesus' story, God's kingdom has become a safe place for generations of believers.

What is the wisdom of Jesus in this case? It is that no one should underestimate the growth of the kingdom of God. Whether in regard to an individual's life, or in society at large, the "seed" of faith and its initial growth may be imperceptible for a period of time. But its eventual impact in transforming people's lives will be surprisingly significant.

Who's Looking?

In Jesus' time, piety was appraised through prayer, fasting, and almsgiving or charity. It was possible to put on the mask of piety by praying fervently in public, or carrying fasting to an extreme, or making great displays of generosity. While the artifice of such performances impressed others, the unanswered question concerned what good was done for the soul.

Beware of practicing your piety before others in order to be seen by them; for then you have no reward from your Father in heaven.

Matthew 6:1

I have come to the hermitage on retreat. In this small cabin, all my needs are met: food and water, light, warmth, toilet facilities, books, a comfortable bed, table and chair. Absent are the distractions of telephone and TV. Though isolated in a wooded environment, I can relax, knowing I am but a short distance from those on duty in the office. I have come here to

spend time with God. Alone, in such a private place, how do I pray?

Do I spend hours on my knees, reading the formal prayers of others? Do I call aloud to God—and wait quietly for an answer? Do I sing, worshiping God with word and song and breath? Do I stand, arms heavenward, in a timeless posture of prayer? Do I walk in the woods, seeking God in creation? Do I dance, praising the Cosmic Dancer with my entire body? Do I talk to God as I would to my closest friend?

Or do I lie on the bed, silently raising mind and heart to God? Or, in absolute awe before my Creator, do I lie prone on the floor? Or sit cross-legged on the floor in meditation?

How does my piety express itself here, in this isolated space, where I am seen and heard by God alone? Would I pray differently here than in public? Does it make a difference? To others? To me? To God?

God,
Hear my prayers. Help me keep my prayers directed at you—not at people I'm trying to impress with my piety. Give me the courage to explore creative ways to speak to you. Thank you God for listening to me.
Amen

Practicing Hospitality

With a humble heart and the Bible's encouragement, we can reach out to welcome children, others, and ourselves.

Then he took a little child and put it among them;
and taking it in his arms, he said to them, "Whoever
welcomes one such child in my name welcomes me,
and whoever welcomes me welcomes not me
but the one who sent me."

Mark 9:36–37

There are often many layers of meaning to a simple act. Jesus welcomes a child, which is a way of eventually welcoming God. The simplest deeds of kindness and hospitality have deep meanings.

Begin with welcoming a child. Jesus' act has great importance in our society, where children are often ignored or neglected. In our fast-paced world, many do not have time or take time to play with children. We are too busy to squat down and listen to a child, especially if they are not our own. Teachers are still underpaid and funding for education in most states is a constant uphill battle. We still have homeless and hungry children in our country.

Jesus and the children

Jesus embraced a child; he welcomed children into the circle of adults. Children have something to teach us. A family with an autistic son has just started coming to our church. One Sunday, at the beginning of the worship service, the son walked up the center aisle and blew out the candles on the altar. I was pleased that no one got upset at this strange action. A fourth-grade boy got up to help me relight the candles. He said, "It is all right. It's my birthday, and he just blew out the candles early." I was touched by the wise, accepting comment from the boy and the gracious understanding of the congregation. When we welcome children, we will be surprised and blessed by their deeds and words.

On another level, Jesus is teaching the disciples that hospitality is not just practiced for friends, but it is extended to all, even to the poor and forgotten. In Jesus' day and in ours, children have little influence. They can't advance our careers or create wealth. So Jesus is saying that hospitality is to be extended to those who are children: those without influence or wealth or power.

Angel detail of Joseph's Dream *by Giotto di Bondone*

We are often a fearful society, locking our cars, dead bolting our front doors, and avoiding the eyes of strangers. It is hard for us to have a humble, hospitable heart when we live in fear of others. Can we create a free open space in our hearts and in our homes where we can welcome others who may be different from us?

Hospitality is also laying aside our fears long enough to receive the gifts that the other may bring. It is one of the richest biblical concepts.

In the Old Testament, Abraham welcomed three strangers with a special meal. They turned out to be messengers from God (Genesis 18:1–15). In the New Testament, when two travelers to Emmaus invited the stranger to spend the night, Jesus responded by breaking bread and revealing himself as the risen Christ (Luke 24:13–35). Scripture is full of stories of hospitality that remind us that when we welcome the stranger as a guest, we may be entertaining angels or Christ himself.

Welcome others.
Welcome yourself.
Welcome God.

Such humble hospitality comes from an open heart that trusts God is present in each encounter and is the host of the meeting. We will probably always be a little wary of strangers in our confusing and sometimes violent world, but as we move toward hospitality, we will break down the walls that divide us and create a corner of God's new community of love.

One sign of such hospitality is the groups that encourage travelers to stay in homes when they visit foreign countries. Our family has belonged to an organization called Servas for a number of years, and we have received into our home people from all over the world. We enjoy an evening meal together, provide a place to rest, and share some of what is interesting about our area that they might like to do. With broken bread and sometimes broken English, we have learned about other countries, shared stories, and formed some lasting friendships. Our children correspond with people from Scotland to New Zealand.

Likewise, when we have traveled, we have stayed in people's homes and gotten to know a new place through the eyes of people who live there.

God of love,
Let me see others with the clear eyes of a child.
Let me welcome others with the simple joy of a child.
Let me love others with the warm heart of a child.
Let me worship you with the trusting soul of a child.
And help me remember that I am one of your
   important children.
Thank you God for children.
Amen

We have been blessed to visit people who have stayed in our home. The hospitality of sharing food, conversation, and a place to rest has created ties that cross economic and political boundaries.

Hospitality creates a free space where people can be themselves, can reveal the gifts they have to share. You don't have to be part of any group to begin the practice of hospitality. You can begin by looking around and being present to those you meet. Begin by inviting someone to dinner, or for tea, or to a barbecue. It does require creating some empty space inside yourself so you are not preoccupied with your own agenda, which prohibits good listening.

When we say yes to visitors from another country, or when we invite someone into our house, we are saying we will make time and space for the guest. Often I have to ask myself if I am open to receiving another, am I willing to be affected by their presence. To be truly hospitable is to be fully present.

Jesus would also have us practice hospitality with ourselves. Can we be open to all the parts of our own personality? There are commercial pressures that make us feel less than the gifted person God made us. Can we practice hospitality toward the way we look? Our shyness? Our playfulness? Our worry? Can we welcome the child within us? Such hospitality is a way of being comfortable in our own house, our own skin. When we are at home with ourselves, we can more easily create a hospitable space for others.

A Life of Service

Each of us is called to a life of service. God's voice may sound in our own inner conversations, in encouraging a friend, in hearing a specific need, or in realizing that we have specific skills that could help others. How is God calling you to serve?

He said to them, "Do you know what I have done to you? You call me Teacher and Lord—and you are right, for that is what I am. So if I, your Lord and Teacher, have washed your feet, you also ought to wash one another's feet. For I have set you an example, that you also should do as I have done to you."

John 13:12–15

At the age of 30, Albert Schweitzer was a preacher, teacher, published author, and a world-renowned organist. When he read an article about people dying in French Equatorial Africa (now Gabon), he felt that God was speaking to him as he read. "And you, Albert, would you give up everything to become a doctor and go to Africa?" Schweitzer's call to service led him to six years of medical school, where he specialized in tropical diseases. His fiancee, Hélène Bresslau, spent those years training as a nurse so she could join his efforts in helping the people of Africa.

In 1911, the then 38-year-old man and his wife went to Lambaréné in French Equatorial Africa, where they established a hospital to treat people with malaria, leprosy, yellow fever, and other diseases. Schweitzer persevered in his commitment to the people of Lambaréné despite hardship, two world wars, and separation from his family. Because of his generous giving of himself, Albert Schweitzer received the Nobel Peace Prize in 1952. Albert Einstein called him "the greatest man alive."

Schweitzer's greatness came from his ability to humbly live the life of a servant. He gave up the security of his comfortable life in Europe because he

I don't know what your destiny will be, but one thing I do know: the only ones among you who will be really happy are those who have sought and found how to serve.

Albert Schweitzer

knew he could make a difference in Africa. He understood the Jesus who washed his disciples' feet and said, "For I have set you an example, that you also should do as I have done to you."

We can only imagine the mixture of emotions the disciples felt when their Lord and teacher knelt before them to wash their feet. Peter was especially uncomfortable, protesting, "You will never wash my feet." When Jesus responded, "Unless I wash you, you have no share of me," Peter quickly replied, "Lord, not my feet only but also my hands and my head!"

As confusing as the reversal of roles in that foot washing may have been to Jesus' followers, it has become for Christians an important symbol of who we are: servants of God. We understand ourselves to be like Christ when we offer ourselves to help others, not counting the cost or asking, "How will this look? Is this task worthy of my position? What will I get out of it?"

Since Jesus first made clear the call to discipleship, countless of his followers have discovered their own calling to servanthood. Linda and Millard Fuller answered the call to serve when they founded Habitat for Humanity in 1976. Habitat offers low-income families a chance to own their own home through the efforts of volunteers who build the dwellings with the homeowner. Now, thousands of people around the world have decent housing thanks to the efforts of Habitat for Humanity. Millard and Linda Fuller and countless Habitat volunteers found their way to serve.

Peace Pilgrim set out on foot on January 1, 1953. She walked until her death 28 years later because she felt called by God to a life of spreading the possibility of peace. She walked until she found shelter, fasted until she was offered food, and carried with her only a comb, toothbrush, ballpoint pen, copies of her message about peace, and unanswered mail. Peace Pilgrim walked thousands of miles in all 50 states and Canada because she believed that if everyone had a sense of inner peace, there would no longer be any need of violence or war. Peace Pilgrim found her way to serve.

When 11-year-old Trevor Farrell saw a news broadcast on the homeless in Philadelphia, he was

Do all the good you can,
By all the means you can,
In all the ways you can,
In all the places you can,
At all the times you can,
To all the people you can,
As long as ever you can.

John Wesley

moved to take a blanket from his home to a homeless person on the city streets that very night. Trevor's concern for those who live on the streets led to Trevor's Campaign, involving many other people who donated time, money, warm clothes, food, and blankets to the homeless. Eventually, Trevor's Place, a homeless shelter, was opened in Philadelphia. Trevor Farrell found his way to serve.

Most Christians will find a variety of ways to serve God in their lifetimes. Some people are active in their own congregation, working with young people or missions or the grieving. In addition, many followers of Christ give service to the greater community or world. Jesus' call to serve has many responses as each of us hears, "Do as I have done to you."

Each of us must discern God's call to servanthood. Is your heart touched when you hear a particular need or situation? Perhaps you could offer your time to work with children with cancer or abused animals. Do you want to make a difference globally? Why not link up with a world hunger organization or collect Bibles to send to other countries? Do you have certain skills that might be useful beyond your own profession and family? You might volunteer as treasurer for an environmental organization or offer your legal services to battered women. Do you wonder who in your own neighborhood might use your service? Maybe there's an older adult who needs weekly help buying and transporting groceries. Opportunities for service are endless. Something as simple as spending two hours a week teaching an adult to read could transform that person's life.

If our hearts are open and our spirits generous, serving as Jesus served will give us opportunity after opportunity to experience his love anew as we reach out to others in his name.

You ask me to give you a motto. Here it is: SERVICE. Let this word accompany each of you throughout your life. Let it be ever before you as you seek your way and your duty in the world. May it be recalled to your minds if ever you are tempted to forget it or set it aside. It will not always be a comfortable companion but it will always be a faithful one. And it will be able to lead you to happiness, no matter what the experiences of your lives are. Never have this word on your lips, but keep it in your hearts. And may it be a confidant that will teach you not only to do good but to do it simply and humbly.

Albert Schweitzer

Power Serving

To achieve true greatness, we do not have to misuse or abdicate the power that has been bestowed on us. Rather, we are to use the influence we have to serve God and others.

Jesus called them to him and said, "You know that the rulers of the Gentiles lord it over them, and their great ones are tyrants over them. It will not be so among you; but whoever wishes to be great among you must be your servant."

Matthew 20:25–26

O nce upon a time, an ambassador traveled a long distance to visit a powerful king. He had heard that an alliance with this ruler could provide great benefits to his own country. The reputation of this king's wealth and power was quite well known.

As the ambassador got out of his car at the front door of the king's magnificent palace, he called to the young man under the canopy. "Valet?

Quick, take care of my car. I have important business to attend to with your king!" The young man replied with a snappy, "Yes, sir," as he took the man's car keys.

As the ambassador entered the palace, he was greeted by a woman who explained that the king had prepared a luncheon in honor of his special guest. Her demeanor was pleasant, yet when she asked the ambassador to take a seat in the reception area, he asked, "Don't you have something that's a little more private for distinguished guests?" So she led him down the corridor to a large, more elegant library.

While strolling around the palace grounds before the luncheon, the ambassador saw a groundskeeper trying to remove an old stump. The man was covered with dirt and grime and smelled of sweat. While he pulled and pushed with all his might, the stump wouldn't budge. When the ambassador saw the groundskeeper struggling, he immediately started to help him. But a voice inside him held him back, whispering, "Maintain your dignity, by all means. You don't want to soil this expensive suit."

An hour later, the ambassador was seated in a place of honor at the luncheon table. He heard the doors open and a voice that said, "I'm so glad you could join us." As he stood and turned to greet the king, he felt faint. For as he watched, in walked the valet, the receptionist, and the groundskeeper. But how different they looked! Each was wearing an Armani suit and a large gold ring with the royal crest. They took their seats directly across from him.

The groundskeeper spoke first. "I am the king of this land and these are my children. In fact, everyone in this kingdom is an adopted child with all the rights due a prince or princess." The ambassador finally gathered his wits enough to reply, "If you are all royalty, why did you try to trick me by acting like lower level employees and servants?"

The receptionist/princess answered, "We didn't try to trick you, sir. Everyone in this kingdom is committed to the life of a servant. We are truly royalty, but we serve willingly." "Yes," added the groundskeeper/king, "and all who would ally themselves with us must adopt our practices. Are you willing to join us?"

The ambassador could hardly believe he would be considered a son. His voice cracked as he answered, "Sir, I would love to stay here and learn your ways." "Good," said the king. "We start tomorrow." With a gesture from the king, the valet/prince handed a hanging bag to the ambassador. The king explained, "Here is your royal Armani suit, your ring with my royal crest, your work boots, and ointment for the blisters that you will surely have by this time tomorrow. But perhaps with your help, I can finish removing that stump."

Then they all commenced eating the sumptuous meal that had been prepared, and the ambassador never felt so much at home.

God guarantees all of us opportunities to serve when he indicates that it is not those who abuse their power who will achieve greatness. Instead, the path to becoming great in God's sight is through humbly serving others, a path that even children can follow.

The Agony in the Garden *by Domenikos T. El Greco*

Some of us have gotten the wrong idea about servanthood. We think that to be humble servants we must abdicate our power and influence on others. For example, to be a servant to my employees, must I yield to their pressures for policies that would be unwise for the company? Does a servant attitude demand that I always put

True service comes from a relationship with the divine Other deep inside. We serve out of whispered promptings, divine urgings. Energy is expended but it is not the frantic energy of the flesh.

Richard J. Foster, Celebration of Discipline

activities, committees, and meetings at church before my family's activities? Can I serve if I must also be a leader?

God has called us to be servants and to serve by leading. No greater example of this principle exists than Jesus himself. He did not come into the world to be served, but to serve and give his life as a ransom for our own.

Jesus is the greatest leader who ever walked or served this earth. He served the people who followed him by meeting their physical, emotional, and spiritual needs. He served his disciples by teaching them the Word, telling them powerful stories, and empowering them to go out and share what they had learned with the world. He serves us today as our Savior, high priest, and advocate before God. His greatness is unmatched.

Neither selfish ambition nor resentful service will lead us to greatness. A servantlike attitude of humility must be genuine.

But what would happen if we allowed divine urgings to prompt us into service? What would happen if we decided to use our power and influence to serve our family, friends, coworkers, church, and community?

If we become like Jesus, our wishes for greatness will surely be granted.

Made in God's Image

If there is one virtue that has been both misunderstood and abused throughout the centuries it is this: the virtue of humility.

*All who exalt themselves will be humbled,
and all who humble themselves will be exalted.*

Matthew 23:12

Jesus came to turn our world upside down! He came to teach us to look at people and institutions and God through new lenses. He came to teach us, by his words and his actions, what God, and not humanity, considers the virtuous life.

It is within this context of virtue that Jesus taught us the paradox of pride and humility—where the first shall be last and the last first. How contrary this is to human standards and judgment.

Since this has been difficult for us to accept, we have taken this paradox and often interpreted it for our own purposes. Throughout the history of

Christianity, humility has been misappropriated by the powerful and dominant to quell the rights of others by using the command, "Be humble!" It has been used by races and nationalities and classes and countries to keep others from enjoying freedom or recognizing their own worth or fulfilling their potentials.

Humility has been the excuse given by institutions to keep its members from using their God-given gifts; it has been used by whites to justify keeping people of color in subjugation; it has been used by men to keep women in submission. It has been, and continues to be, called upon by individuals to

keep others in obedience.

None of these instances reflect Jesus' view of humility; none of these instances reflect God's inclusive radical love, which is the source for all creation.

It is easier to describe humility by stating what it is not. Humility is not self-abasement; it is not demeaning. And while honesty demands that we admit both our limitations and our sinfulness, we must also, in truth, recognize our blessed and gifted humanity. Thus, regarding ourselves as worthless or denying our talents is insulting, even blasphemous, to our

Creator, in whose image we have been created.

Neither is humility expressed in prideful self-importance or in placing ourselves above others. Love and truth demand the recognition of the dignity and equality of all people before God.

Humility is always in tension between these two extremes: admission of our flaws and recognition of our graced humanity. Humility thrives in the balance.

Thank you God, for creating ME!
In your womb I have been fashioned;
Your Spirit dwells within me;
Truly I am wonderfully, marvelously made!
From your love and wisdom have I come
To this place and time.
To me you have given talent and life and blessings.
To me you have given tasks given to no others.
With joy and gratitude
I celebrate my much-honored existence.
From ages past to eternity,
I have been included in your divine plan.
Thank you God, for creating ME!

Perhaps humility is more easily recognized by the company it keeps, for that virtue never flourishes alone. Humility is joined by honesty, truthfulness, joy, integrity, a hunger for justice, honor, self-acceptance, love, sincerity, accountability, and, most importantly, a sense of humor.

When Jesus Asks You to Be Wise

❧❧❧

God chose what is foolish in the world to shame the wise; God chose what is weak in the world to shame the strong; God chose what is low and despised in the world, things that are not, to reduce to nothing things that are, so that no one might boast in the presence of God. He is the source of your life in Christ Jesus, who became for us wisdom from God.

1 Corinthians 1:27–30

Wisdom, A New Heart

Jesus challenges the conventional wisdom with a new wisdom of the heart.

*He came to his hometown and began to teach
the people in their synagogue, so that they were
astounded and said, "Where did this man get
this wisdom and these deeds of power?"*

Matthew 13:54

The people of Nazareth had seen Jesus grow up. They knew his mother and father, his brothers and sisters. Matthew reports that they were astounded and then offended. How could someone so ordinary be saying what Jesus said? He was judged by his background, by his family. Yet even though they hated to admit it, Jesus was an amazing teacher.

Jesus was a teacher of wisdom; his words and his life drew people into the presence of God. In Jesus, people could see a glimpse of God. As a teacher of wisdom, he called and challenged people to center their life on God, to trust

that the Maker of the universe was a gracious and
compassionate God. His teaching went against the
common wisdom of his day.

The wisdom of Jesus' day, and even today,
is concerned with personal identity and security.
Wealth and possessions were not only a way to
comfort and ease, but they were also thought to be
a sign that God looked upon you with favor. Jesus
warned of the dangers of riches. "How hard it will
be for those who have wealth to enter the
kingdom of God!" (Mark 10:23). Though Jesus
associated with the rich and had some wealthy
supporters, it is clear that Jesus saw money as a
distraction from living a godly life, and he saw greed

Jesus Teaching in the Synagogue *by
James J. Tissot*

putting blinders on people so they no longer had human compassion. Jesus
presented wisdom that was centered on God and service to others.

In Jesus' day, even religion had become a means to identity and
security. People wanted to be a descendant of Abraham and live according to
the rules. The Pharisees thought they were models of religious life because
they faithfully adhered to the most rigorous standards of the day. Yet Jesus
often criticized the Pharisees because their security was based in their own

religious accomplishments. In contrast, Jesus lifted up the example of the tax collector who prayed, "God, be merciful to me, a sinner!" (Luke 18:13).

The wisdom that Jesus brought centered on the heart, the deepest center of a person. The religious externals were less important than the motivations. "Blessed are the pure in heart, for they will see God" (Matthew 5:8).

Dear God,
Give me a new heart that is led
by your wisdom, not the world's
wisdom. Help me see that your
bounty is more valuable than
any wealth I could accumulate.
Teach me to be pure in heart.
Amen

The wisdom of Jesus centered on God. A radical trust in God is contrasted with the anxiety of trying make it on our own. Jesus invited his followers to let go of worry about food, possessions, and security. He asked them to surrender their lives to God. He invited his followers to see that at the heart of everything is a God who loves us. Trust God.

For his friends in Nazareth, the invitation from Jesus was intriguing and frightening. They could see his wisdom, but they knew the security of possessions and of following the religious leaders. They had their families to think of and their careers to advance. Could they trust God to provide?

We wrestle today with the same invitation. Jesus asks us, "Where is your heart?" Do our activities flow from the center of God's grace and guidance?

A Model for Balanced Growth

When a person's thinking and actions become clearly irrational or delusional, that individual is considered imbalanced. Oddly, though, you rarely hear discussed what is meant by balanced. Is there a clear model available that embodies such balance?

*And Jesus increased in wisdom and
in years, and in divine and human favor.*

Luke 2:52

*W*hen a tire on your car is out of balance, the car does not run smoothly. If the tire is not worked on to bring it back into balance, it will wear out (or blow out!) much more quickly than the others. This illustration can help us understand balanced living. Your life is like a tire because it must be balanced to flow smoothly. Like spokes on a wheel, there are at least four areas of life that need to be in balance: the intellectual, the physical, the spiritual, and the social. To the extent that any of these four is out of whack, life begins to get bumpy and may soon break down.

Jesus is history's classic example of balanced growth. To be sure, as the Son of God, he was already perfect and no growth was required. But the humanity of Jesus was not just an illusion or a front. He was just as much human (despite never having sinned) as he was divine. And, as a human being, he grew.

That growth is perceived most easily in the physical realm. Jesus was born to Mary and Joseph as a healthy human baby, then he went through all the normal stages of growth to adulthood. There is no indication that Jesus was in any way out of the ordinary during those years of physical growth.

Jesus Among the Doctors *(teachers) by Jean Auguste Dominique Ingres*

Jesus also grew in the intellectual sense. A stunning example of this took place when Jesus was 12 years old and he went with Joseph and Mary to a feast in Jerusalem. He astounded the Jewish

Lord,
I admit that my life is not
as balanced as it should
be. Grant me the wisdom
to develop a life that is
well rounded in your eyes.
Amen

teachers in the temple with his grasp of Scripture. Yet, as much as he already understood, we are told Jesus still grew in wisdom.

These two dimensions, the physical and intellectual, comprise personal growth. Divine and human favor speak of interpersonal growth. Just as physical and intellectual growth are necessary for a balanced life, so are spiritual and social growth. However, they are more difficult to get a handle on.

There is evidence that Jesus grew in these last two areas also. In the spiritual realm, he made prayer the highest priority. For example, Jesus prayed all night before he chose the 12 apostles. Then, in the Garden of Gethsemane, he struggled in prayer in order to finally accept the Father's will that he die on the cross.

Socially, Jesus also built close relationships. He was very close to Mary, his mother. His closest friends were the inner circle of the apostles: Peter, James, and John. Beyond them, and the rest of the 12, were close male and female friends.

Since Jesus is God, perhaps growth in these areas was easier for him. Jesus was the perfect role model. We can live balanced lives by choosing to pursue intellectual, physical, spiritual, and social development everyday.

Putting Words in Your Mouth

One of life's biggest fears is that when we have to face a frightening event that requires an immediate response, we will simply freeze up and not know what to say or do. Wouldn't it be wonderful to know that the wisdom to handle the situation will be there when you need it?

This will give you an opportunity to testify. So make up your minds not to prepare your defense in advance; for I will give you words and a wisdom that none of your opponents will be able to withstand or contradict.

Luke 21:13–15

The phrase, "putting words in my mouth," is usually used when someone is complaining. It means someone is misrepresenting what the person really wants to say.

In effect, the idea of putting words in someone else's mouth is accusing someone of being a ventriloquist. You open your mouth, but the words that emerge are not really your own. You can end up mouthing the wording provided by the other party.

All of this sounds pretty diabolical. But there is at least one case in which "putting words in your mouth" could be a very positive thing.

Under religious persecution, people are called and asked to defend their beliefs. They can be faced with suffering, imprisonment, or even death if they don't respond as the persecutors want them to. The very way things are handled is a calculated attempt to unnerve or terrify the person on trial. If the strategy is successful, the defendants may provide crucial information or even recant their beliefs.

Perhaps the biggest difficulty in attempting to survive this kind of trial is that the person is separated from others. As long as there is a support system, most people can withstand a great deal. But if you feel isolated and all alone, it is much harder to take the pressure.

While persecution or other trials may seem to leave you all alone, that is not the case. The Lord has promised, "I will never leave you or forsake you"; his spiritual presence is always present. But he has also made another incredible promise: He will, somehow, put the right words in your mouth, at the right time, in order for you to defend yourself.

Now, that does not mean that close-minded opposition will be satisfied with what is said. But it does mean that God's viewpoint will get presented powerfully enough to impact someone who is present with an open mind.

History is full of examples of those who did not think they could speak up under such difficult circumstances. Then, when the time came, they heard their own voices speaking eloquent words that were at once their own, yet seemed to come from another source, a higher power.

Lord,
The very thought of having to stand up and
answer for my faith terrifies me. Thank you for
promising to provide the wisdom needed, should
I have to face such an ordeal.
Amen

Being placed on the firing line to defend your faith is not something that most people look forward to. Yet, if it were to happen, it is a great comfort to know that the Lord would provide the wisdom needed to respond properly, at just the right time.

Like a Little Child

The followers of Jesus in this passage were not the most important people of their nation. Nor were they considered the "wise" or "intelligent." Rather, God revealed his great mysteries to those who became like little children.

At that time Jesus said, "I thank you, Father, Lord of heaven and earth, because you have hidden these things from the wise and the intelligent and have revealed them to infants; yes, Father, for such was your gracious will."

Matthew 11:25–26

Do you remember Hans Christian Andersen's fairy tale *The Emperor's New Clothes*? The emperor heard that two weavers could make clothes that had the peculiarity of being invisible to anyone who was hopelessly stupid. Hoping to identify the clever statesmen from the stupid in his court, the emperor hired the weavers to design an elaborate new outfit for him to wear in a procession through the village.

All the emperor's officials, prime ministers, gentlemen-in-waiting, and chamberlains dared not let it be known that they couldn't see any clothes. Even the emperor was afraid to admit that he couldn't see anything. Thus the emperor proceeded through the town stark naked. But one small child in the crowds cried out, "But he hasn't got anything on." The whispering began and spread until the crowd was shouting, "He hasn't got anything on!"

With that innocent observation, a small child revealed the truth about the emperor's invisible wardrobe.

Children often exhibit simple wisdom. They catch us off guard by stating or doing the obvious when we adults are experiencing either fear or embarrassment.

Take my friend Marie, a wonderfully perceptive seven year old who dreams of someday becoming a great archaeologist or missionary—or both! A

GREAT GOD OF ALL WISDOM

Great God of all wisdom, of science and art,
O grant us the wisdom that comes from the heart.
Technology, learning, philosophy, youth—
All leave us still yearning for your word of truth.
Creator of visions as well as of stars,
O mend our divisions and heal all our scars.
You reign over history, both present and past,
Most challenging mystery from first to the last.

Jane Parker Huber

highly imaginative child, Marie intuitively seems to know how to help others dream as well. As I listen to her sincere prayers before meals, it is clear that her heart has been softened by the Holy Spirit. I am struck by her sensitivity to the needs of her friends, family, and neighbors, even those hurting and in distress around the world.

During the winter months when the youth ministry group sponsored by her mom volunteered to serve meals to the homeless, Marie asked if she could tag along. With her mom's permission, Marie dressed in her best pink leotard and tutu. Because she was too small to ladle soup or serve coffee, she offered all those gathered in the warm church an unusual gift—a ballet of her own creation.

Like a little elf, Marie twirled and leaped, humming under her breath as her long blonde hair flowed behind her. An old man wrapped in a bulky tweed coat and a single mother with small children smiled as the animated little girl spun across the room with effortless grace. The folks huddled over their hot food, but they couldn't help but notice the little blonde fairy darting around the room.

Even the members of the student ministry team stopped to watch the little ballerina entertain her audience. With the bleakness of the winter winds howling outside, Marie's wise, unselfish act of service was refreshing to the heart and not unlike King David's dance (see 2 Samuel 6:14). How like a little child to lead us in understanding the special, unseen needs of others!

No matter how wise or smart we are, no matter how old we are, we will never be able to understand everything about heaven, humankind, or this galaxy in which we live. God has hidden the great mysteries of his wisdom from all of us, particularly from those of us who consider ourselves to be wise and educated. Instead he chooses to whom he will reveal the truths of how we should live, and sometimes he does so through the simplest means—the words and actions of a little child like Marie.

The one thing we can understand is that gaining wisdom can only be experienced by those who come to God in childlike faith. And as we become like children—observant, intuitive, uninhibited, sensitive, giving, caring, jubilant—he receives us with joy and delights in us as he imparts his wisdom.

Index